The God of the Cruel World

The God of the Cruel World

Five tough questions about God, the world and suffering

Bob Eckhard

The God of the Cruel World
© 2007 Bob Eckhard

ISBN: 978-0-9556795-0-6

Creevagh Books
PO Box 47270
London W7 1WG
United Kingdom

Further copies of this book may be ordered from Lulu Publishing and other online bookstores. Information and a link to these sites is available through

www.toughquestions.org

*To my mother, who taught me
the value of a good question*

Contents

Acknowledgements   9

Introduction   11

Part 1 – Towards Discussion

1   Tough Questions Forum   19

2   Advice to the Individual Reader   23

3   Leading Discussion Groups   29

Part 2 – Five Tough Questions

4   Moral Evil   39
      (Why doesn't God remove evil people from the world?)

5   Natural Evil   51
      (Why does God allow natural disasters to occur?)

6   Death and Illness   71
      (Why did my friend have to die?)

7   World Religions   85
      (Do all religions lead to God?)

8   Invisible God   101
      (Is it possible to prove God's existence?)

Part 3 – Thinking Ahead

9	Not a Conclusion	117
10	Postscript	121
11	Reflection Sheets	127
12	Questions for Group Discussion	139
13	Further Reading and Research	145
14	References	146

Acknowledgements

There are a number of people who need to be mentioned here. Colleagues, lecturers, students, friends and associates have all helped in the development of my thinking over the years. Sometimes the contribution has been apparent, for example when someone has challenged me to rethink my understanding by arguing against something I have said. Other times, the contribution has been less obvious in that it was simply a question or encouragement from a friend that caused me to think around the issue at greater length – the results of which are to be found in the pages of this book.

I would also like to express a particular debt of thanks to the Rev Dr Tim Hull for his friendship and inspired teaching in regard to this subject, helping me to think through some of the more complex theological ideas and arguments that would have otherwise befuddled me altogether. I am also grateful for his feedback and ideas for my earlier talks on the Tough Questions Forum and for his encouragements with this book – a book which finds its way into your hand through the generous efforts of Ben Williams and Martin Wroe who guided me through the process of internet publishing with respect to producing the cover and written material. A special thank you also goes to Fiona Campbell and Abigail Frymann for their help in editing the material.

Lastly, I would like to thank all the people who have attended the forum over the years and have contributed to the development of the material in this book through the ideas they brought to the discussion. My gratitude also goes to the staff team at St Paul's Church Ealing in West London and the community for all their encouragement and prayers. This includes Mark Melluish for the opportunity to develop the Tough Questions ministry and those who have helped lead these forums, particularly Jenny, Marcelo, Fadi, Tim, Jon and Fiona. For all your help and support in this ongoing adventure – thank you.

Introduction

Sunday School Teacher: *'What has a large bushy tail, climbs trees, and stores its food during winter?'*

Child: *'Well ... its sounds awfully like a squirrel ... but I'm guessing the answer is Jesus.'*

I start with this joke because I think it illustrates a problem that is endemic to the majority of churches in the Western world – a problem that is so ingrained in many believers that they are not even aware of it when it happens. It has found its way into a huge amount of contemporary Christian literature and is prevalent at many of the conferences I attend. I refer of course to the 'glib' Christian answer! An answer that is reeled off without thought as to how it addresses the person's question or what was really being asked between the lines. Like a child who has rehearsed a poem for performance but neither understands its content or the meter within it, such are the answers that the believing community give to people outside the church who ask tough questions of them. In short, 'Jesus' has become the answer to every question that might possibly be asked. And great answer that it is, quite frankly, it's not enough.

Now, it will help to state right away that I am a follower of Jesus Christ. I am also an ordained minister in the Church of England who desires to see church communities everywhere think through and explore the questions that people have in order that they might provide real and helpful answers – answers that are not some form of rehearsed doctrinal mantra telling the person to 'just believe' or informing them of how some things are a 'holy mystery' that must remain unknown. Such answers provide no real help or comfort to people who are wrestling with questions about how a loving God can allow suffering in the world. The instruction to 'just believe' is absolute nonsense because it does not take into account the experiences of the questioner prior to that moment – experiences such as a baby being miscarried, a friend murdered, a child born blind, a parent affected by a debilitating illness, a relative killed in an earthquake. To the person involved, this suggests that the world is not such a pleasant place to live, and by inference, the Creator is not good and loving.

In an attempt to provide better answers to questions about God, the world and suffering, the Tough Questions Forum was set up in January 2005. Initially this was a pilot project I devised for my final year presentation at college. It consisted of a short series of talks aimed at people in my church who I thought would enjoy the opportunity to engage with these questions. Among this group were a number who I knew were reluctant to attend church while their issues with God remained unresolved. A group who considered God cruel and vindictive because of the various atrocities they witnessed in the world. A

Introduction

position that can only change as sceptic and believer engage with one another in real and honest debate.

Since that time, the Tough Questions Forum has developed in a number of ways. Firstly, it has extended into a five week course that runs regularly at St Paul's and other churches around the country. Secondly, the talks have been adapted and used within the church's midweek groups to help people process these issues for themselves. Lastly, the forum has helped many people to reflect on what they believe about God in the light of these questions, challenging their understanding of the how, when, and why God chooses to work in our world.

It will be clear from what I have written here that I am not without bias myself. My own personal belief is that God has been misrepresented over the years by church communities who have failed to tackle these issues in a way that explains the Divine within the essence of good and loving behaviour. Often, it seems as if the church is conspicuously silent about God when things happen in the world that challenge orthodox ideas about the Divine – possibly fearing the sceptic's reasoning that if God knew a disaster was going to happen, why didn't God act to stop it?

It will help at this point if I say a little bit about the book itself. My intention in writing it is that it should be as accessible to the sceptic as much as it is to the believer. Hopefully, this is reflected in the way the chapters look objectively at each topic and address the issues involved. Likewise, I have also approached this book with the novice in mind, so it is designed for people who come to the subject with limited theological understanding. Indeed, wherever possible I have taken care not to use complex vocabulary as I am aware that sometimes the ideas themselves can be complicated enough to grapple with. That said, although I have made some attempt to address each question, I am aware that there will be a whole number of other ideas and answers that I have not considered. Indeed, it is not my intention to produce a book that provides every answer to these five questions: I do not believe this is possible. If you are seeking such a book you will find many produced by Christian writers, though it is my contention that these may simply reference unchallenged orthodox ideas and answers. Rather, my intention is to lay a foundation on which people might engage with these issues in a real and challenging way. Of course, some people will want to research these questions further and I will make some suggestions as to how to go about this in the last chapter.

Editorially, I have taken care to avoid using quotes and references wherever possible as my intention is to produce a book that is readable rather than largely academic. I have also tried my best to avoid using the male pronoun to reference God because I appreciate that some people will have difficulty with referencing the Divine in this way. Although I have had some success with avoiding masculine pronouns, it has been necessary to use them in certain places rather than lose

Introduction

the meaning of the sentence for the sake of a misplaced word. Throughout the piece you may also note that I have taken care to avoid using scripture verses and the reason for this is explained in chapter 3 ('Two Rules').

Lastly, I anticipate that some people may have difficulty with the title of this book because it challenges orthodox ideas about God creating a perfect world. If you are offended by this, please do try and understand that it is not my intention to write a book that will only appeal to believers, but to those whose experience of God is wholly different; by this I mean people whose thinking about God resonates with what is read on the cover because they do not consider the Divine to be good or loving, because the world is flawed and cruel.

So what of the five questions that we shall consider in the following chapters? Well, four of them have been developed from talks used on the Tough Questions Forum. The other is a completely new talk which looks at issues that are connected with death and illness. The five questions mirror what people ask me from time to time. These questions may hinder people's understanding of God as good and loving, and (dare I say it?) are the five most important issues that the church should be addressing today. My hope is that you will find the book both challenging and enjoyable. Moreover, I hope it might aid you in your search for better answers to the questions you have about God, the world and suffering. All the best!

Part 1
Towards Discussion

1   Tough Questions Forum

Let me begin by saying this book is the product of The Tough Questions Forum – a five-week course which began three years ago to encourage people to come together to discuss difficult questions about God, the world and suffering. Although my intention at that time was to develop a project suitable for my final year presentation at theological college, it soon became clear that the topics and format of the course appealed to many people inside and outside of the church. People whose unresolved issues with God were not always addressed in the structure of other courses such as Alpha where two assumptions are made from the start: God exists and God is loving to all he has made. These two assumptions can be a real challenge to rational thinkers who question how people can believe this when faced with the turmoil and destruction of the world around them.

Although I know that Alpha has helped many people, I am also aware (from my experience of helping to lead this course) that it can disappoint some who do not continue to attend after the first couple of weeks. Often, these people arrive with their own questions in mind and become frustrated when the presented subject matter does not 'scratch' where they 'itch'. Moreover, they may also discover that their questions often stand outside of what some in the believing community are prepared to engage with and discuss.

The God of the Cruel World

Questions such as:

Why doesn't God do something about evil people in the world?
Why does God allow natural disasters to occur?
Why did my friend have to die?
Do all religions lead to God?
Is it possible to prove God's existence?

Having spoken with a number of sceptics over the years, I have reached the conclusion that most of them are genuinely seeking answers to these perplexing questions. If anything, they often reveal a greater degree of integrity in their questioning because they are reluctant to accept a model of God which they believe is compromised by evil and suffering in the world – issues that believers remain quite comfortable with even though they have little or no ability to adequately explain the apparent contradiction to others. But back to the forum and the format of the course!

It is necessary to say that because the Tough Questions Forum happens in a number of churches, I cannot be certain how it operates within each particular context because it may have been adapted to meet needs in different ways. However, what I can say is that in our church, the sessions usually start with a short time for refreshments. After this, a member of the team gives a presentation on one of the five issues. The remainder of the session is given over to small-group discussion as people offer their own thoughts on what they have heard and any other ideas they have about the subject matter. It is at this point that the fun really begins as people debate the issues in the light of what they believe. From feedback with people who have attended these courses it is apparent that although many would say they find the presentations interesting and challenging, the greatest benefit comes from the opportunity the forum provides to discuss these ideas with others.

In educational terms, this is the social constructivist model of learning in which people advance their understanding through engaging others in discussion. This engagement requires a degree of openness from each person as they elect to be verbally explicit about what they actually believe in order that others may challenge what has been said. This group discussion works well if arranged in such a way that there is a good mix of people who are different in terms of what they understand, and the contrary values/beliefs they may hold.

As I will explain the management of the group more fully (in chapter 3), I will close here with the observation that we have found the Tough Questions Forum to be a useful tool in helping sceptics and believers to engage with these issues. So useful in fact, that it has led me to write this book in order that others might look into these issues, reflect, and advance in their understanding. With these processes in mind, consider next some ideas for how the individual reader might make best use of this book.

2 Advice to the Individual Reader

I have a strong desire to apologise as I write this section, possibly because I am aware that people will not take kindly to being given guidance on how to read and process material in a book. If that is you, please do bear with me as I would like to say a little bit about 'self-reflection' – a discipline that is sadly absent in our world today, largely due to busy lifestyles, but sometimes because people have not been coached in this process.

There is not enough space here to provide a complete training in self-reflection, and there are others who are far better qualified than me who can do this for you. However, what I would like to do is introduce you to an idea that has developed in recent years – that of 'dialectical voice'. This is a concept more often associated with the process of writing, particularly the act of journaling ideas onto paper. In essence, it is the voice inside our head that argues, cajoles, encourages, disputes with us over what finds its way onto paper as ideas are scribbled out and new words overlaid, until we are content with what has been written. A good example might be the times when we have to write a difficult letter to someone and desire the content to be constructive and sensitive. On these occasions, the voice within our head becomes the second person who advises us on what words to use and the sentiment that finds its way into the final draft.

I would like to take this idea of dialectical thinking a little bit further because I believe this occurs more frequently than we actually realise. You see, in the same way that the dialectical voice can aid us when we write, it also seems to be the voice inside our head which reminds us to take the keys as we leave the house. The same voice which advises us to reason through the decision we are about to make and the ramifications of taking one action over and against another. It is the voice that argues with us over which present we should buy for a friend. In short, it is the voice of the second person inside each of us who may at one moment challenge us over something we have decided to do, while on another confirm that the decision we have just made is the correct one. This voice counsels us against the excess of impetuosity in the things we write, but is also a safeguard in regard to the things we say and do – of course, this is a whole lot easier in theory than in practice!

Next, let me introduce another idea of the 'dialectic' which is most commonly associated with the German philosopher Georg Wilhelm Friedrich Hegel (though it is more likely that it was developed by others before him). Basically, this model of thinking considers how a greater understanding of a subject may be obtained by investigating the contrary ideas associated with it. Although this process sounds complicated, it is really quite straightforward and involves three stages of thought:

- Thesis   (a proposition or theory)
- Antithesis (a proposition that counters it)
- Synthesis   (the reconciliation of ideas into a new truth)

It will be helpful to use an example to illustrate how this dialectic works. Suppose a woman has a theory that only green apples exist in the world. She reaches this conclusion because the country where she lives only produces green apples. However, one day, while on holiday in another country, she meets a different woman who believes that only red apples exist. Moreover, this woman produces a red apple for her and cuts it open so that she can see that it is the same, except for the fact that its peel is a different colour. The first woman is now forced to reconsider her original theory and revise it in the light of this new evidence to conclude a new truth: 'all apples are green or red'. Actually, the second woman also has to revise her theory about red apples. The synthesis of the two ideas forms a new theory that will exist until such time that a different apple is introduced to counter and revise this further – say, a yellow apple. Now, in terms of our dialectic, what we see is this:

- Thesis   (all apples are green)
- Antithesis (all apples are red)
- Synthesis   (all apples are green or red)

The new proposition is arrived at through the reconciliation of two conflicting truths which becomes the synthesis of these ideas. But what has all this got to do with self-reflection and reading this book?

Well, because this is a book and not a discussion group, there is no requirement for the individual reader to be explicit about what they consider truth because there is no person challenging them with contrary ideas or explanations. Quite simply, there is no opportunity for 'antithesis' to occur because the reader does not engage with others who might disagree with what they believe or suggest. All of this means that if the individual is going to interact properly with these new ideas in any sort of discursive way, they must first become proactive in the self-reflective process through the development of the 'dialectic' and 'dialectical voice'.

With this in mind, you will find in the back section of the book (chapter 11) some reflection sheets for you to journal your thoughts. Ideally, these reflection sheets should be used in advance of any reading of the main questions section so that you are clear about your own thinking on the subject beforehand. Later, having read the respective chapter, you can record your reflections again, this time in the light of different theories that you may have found challenging to what you believe. The idea is to become explicit about what you think in advance of what you read.

So, should you believe that God is responsible for natural disasters you record this on the reflection sheet (and it becomes 'thesis'). Once the section on 'Natural

Advice to the Individual Reader

Evil' has been read, you may come to the conclusion that there is compelling evidence that you have never considered before and these ideas are recorded on the page opposite (as 'antithesis'). Lastly, as you attempt to resolve the two aspects (thesis and antithesis) it is likely that you will arrive at a better understanding of the issue (synthesis). In this instance, what you now understand about God and natural disasters. Throughout this process, the second person (or dialectical voice) is the guide who helps you wrestle with the ideas you are prepared to consider and revise on paper. These ideas will help you think through the issues so that you may reach a more complete proposition.

Obviously, there is great value in taking time to discuss these ideas with people who think differently to you – I advise you to talk to people who are different because there is no discord between two musical notes that sound the same. However, in the absence of finding someone to talk with about the material in this book, I do believe that the reflection tool that I have outlined will assist you to process these issues in a constructive way. In the next chapter I will give a few guidelines to people who are looking at these issues as part of a small discussion group. But for those of you who are tackling the book by yourself, you might want to skip the next chapter and start on the questions. However, don't forget to record your initial thoughts about each of the five questions in the reflection sheet section.

3 Leading Discussion Groups

Although some people will need little guidance in leading a discussion group, you may find it useful to read this section in order to avoid the mistakes that we have made on the Tough Questions Forum over the years – and we have made quite a few! The other reason I would suggest reading this chapter is that I will outline two different models for leading a discussion group, which is dependent on the mix of people you anticipate attending. These being:

- A mixed group (of sceptics and believers)
- A group of believers

1 Mixed group

Let me state straight away that mixed groups are what the Tough Questions Forum is all about, because here sceptics and believers wrestle with these issues from different perspectives. Consequently, it can also be quite problematic in that it brings together two sets of people who want to vigorously defend their ideas and arguments – possibly because their identity and *raison d'être* are also at stake. This can lead very quickly to tension rising within the group as people keep to their respective positions in ways that are not conducive to free and constructive discussion.

Reflecting on this problem, it was realised early on that while it was not possible to manage every outcome of the discussion group, it was possible to minimise some points of contention. A major contention was that most members saw themselves as the nominated defender of their respective idea or faith - a position which inevitably led to both sceptic and believer becoming reluctant to consider other people's ideas or different propositions because they feared, if they did, they would be conceding too much. With this problem in mind, some ground rules were introduced into the forum to establish boundaries for people. Two rules designed to enable open discussion to happen by managing the main contentions that sceptics and believers have with one another. These rules are still considered to be the lynch-pin of what enables discussion to happen on The Tough Questions Forum.

The sceptic-believer compromise: two rules

At the start of every course, two rules are explained to the group – one rule for the sceptic and the other for the believer. Each week, the group is reminded about these rules and how they facilitate a level playing field during the discussion time. Although a few people have, on occasions, had difficulty with the restrictions placed on them, it does seem that most find this sceptic-believer compromise to be beneficial because it enables a more rounded discussion to develop.

First rule

The first is geared towards those who would actively describe themselves as believers. Here I am particularly thinking of people who would admit to having faith in God or Jesus Christ, and an absolute certainty regarding the claims of the Bible. (For the remainder of this book I will refer to them as 'believers'). Particular to this type of faith is the believer's reliance on what is written in Holy Scripture, using the Bible to justify a particular viewpoint of God or explain something that has happened in the world in terms of an unseen theological implication.

Although many believers use verses from scripture to help explain the activity or inactivity of God in the world, it is necessary to note that to sceptics and rational thinkers outside of the church, such behaviour is absolute nonsense.

Central to the sceptic's discomfort with scripture is the observation that believers appear to behave irrationally by making outrageous claims about the Bible and how the authority of God is contained within the pages of a book. Moreover, as the sceptic has difficulty with any sort of belief in God, it should come as no surprise that the specific claims of the Bible are held in even lesser regard. Given the difficulties between sceptic and believer regarding the validity and authority of scripture, the first rule centres on creating a way in which the discussion may be facilitated in a manner accessible to both positions.

With this in mind, the requirement is that believers should reference God out of their experience rather than what they understand through scripture – a rule that guards against the possible misuse of scripture by believers who defend an untenable position by using the Bible as if it were some sort of 'trump card'. For example, statements from believers who assert something like: 'I know God loves me because it says so in the Bible' is a theoretical statement. Far better the person gives a practical example of how they have experienced God's love in their lives by recounting something like 'I know God loves me because when I was bereaved, people prayed for me and I had a sense of comfort and peace.'

First rule

Believers do not reference the Bible to support the point they are making but rather speak from a position of what they have already personally experienced.

Second rule

This rule requires a concession from the sceptic to resist the rationalist loop-hole which allows statements to be made at the end of each discussion that states something like: 'Well, since God doesn't exist, any argument is hypothetical anyway!' Instead, the requirement on the sceptic is that a presumption be made (for the duration of the discussion) that a higher life form does exist, which is beyond human and rational experience. A force or 'thing' that may be held attributable for the building blocks of life today so as not to pander to simplistic philosophies and ideologies that reduce God to little more than a human idea. Of course, this requires the sceptic to suspend disbelief for a time in order that a different truth might emerge. In terms of the Tough Questions Forum, I often introduce this rule by explaining that we are going to presume that God exists in order to make the Divine Being accountable for evil and suffering in the world. After all, isn't this people's main complaint against a loving God when things go horribly wrong in our world?

Second rule

Sceptics will suspend disbelief and presume that a higher life form exists which is beyond human and rational experience.

Choosing leaders for mixed groups

With the two rules outlined, I would like to conclude with some advice in regard to the choice of leader for a mixed group of sceptics and believers. Now, there is a risk that I will offend someone by what I suggest next, but generally I find that the best people to lead these groups are those who are not too precious about their faith. By this I mean leaders who are not so dogmatic in what they believe that they are thrown into a dizzy spin by other people's ideas which may challenge their understanding about God and the world. My own preference is for leaders who I know will seek out the ideas and thoughts of everyone in the discussion group, irrespective of whether these are at odds with what they might personally think and believe. I also prefer leaders who are confident enough in their faith and understanding that they are able to comfortably undertake (in the absence of a protagonist in the group) a contrary role and argue against what they personally believe so that discussion and debate may occur.

At the end of the book (chapter 13), I have written up a few questions on each of the five issues that might be helpful for starting discussion in groups. My own belief is that the best questions are likely to come from the group members themselves. I would counsel that you consider these issues rather than slavishly work through what I have written – the questions I have suggested are purely there as a way of starting conversation with the group. Of course, the leader will need to take care to ensure that the questions which arise from the group do not wander too far away from the issue that is being discussed. Other than that, I usually find people have more than enough of their own ideas and thoughts to ensure debate is lively and engaging.

2 Church discussion groups

The type of discussion that occurs in this setting is different to the mixed group in a number of ways. One reason for this is that because the discussion occurs in the context of a small study group, it is quite likely that all of the people attending will be known to one another. Moreover, if they attend the same church, it is also reasonable to think that they may also share a similar understanding about God (though this is not always so). Lastly, because most people are likely to agree on the majority of issues, the group will not engage in the same contentious debating that might happen if an atheist were in attendance.

From this, two things are immediately apparent. Firstly, the leader has a responsibility to ensure that the group does not reach a cosy consensus about an issue because there was no other person there to provide an alternative perspective (antithesis). Where no protagonist is available I believe that this becomes the leader's responsibility, but only where enough is known about the subject that they are able to argue an opposing view or ask challenging questions of the group.

Secondly, the earlier restriction that was placed on the believer (in the context of mixed-group discussion) is no longer relevant because we can presume that no-one will have difficulty with the authority of scripture. (That said, some believers might still want to debate how scripture is best interpreted and understood). Interestingly, the lifting of this restriction also enables believers to consider these issues in a completely different way by looking at how events (like earthquakes, illness, and suffering) are understood within the Bible. My only caution here is that both leader and group need to be aware of how the first eleven chapters of Genesis require it to be better understood as 'narrative' so that it is not viewed in a purely chronological or literal way. For example, do we really believe that grass can grow on molten lava as a timeline of a six day Creation would suggest?

Again, the questions at the back of the book will be useful for beginning discussion though I would suggest the leader of the group research scriptural references beforehand so that they can then be brought to the group for consideration. I am envisaging that groups will use the materials in advance of the meeting, reading the chapter before attending the group. The discussion groups then meet to discuss the chapter that has been read during the week. Of course, there is no hard and fast way of using the book. My only hope is that you will enjoy engaging with the discussions which begin now with the issue of moral evil.

Part 2
Five Tough Questions

4 Moral Evil
Why doesn't God do something about evil people in the world?

A bomb explodes in Baghdad killing scores of people and injuring others. Terrorists lay siege to a school in Russia taking children and teachers hostage. Refugees are murdered in Darfur by Sudanese forces and Janjaweed militia. Women are kidnapped and trafficked into the UK to serve as sex slaves in the prostitution industry. A teenager is stabbed and dies on the street of a UK city.

These are just a few of the events that have made our news over the past five years. These stories reveal that moral evil – by this I mean human beings treating others in an evil way – is as prevalent in our society as it has ever been during other periods of our history. The only difference is that with the advancement of communication technologies and global perspectives, there is now an immediate awareness of these horrific events as they happen around the world in a way that was previously unavailable to other generations.

Given the frequency of acts of moral evil in our society today, let us progress our discussion on to the main question of this chapter about why it is that God doesn't do something about evil. Or as people often ask: why doesn't God just come down and sort out all the bad people in our world? Of course, behind this question is a rather simplistic idea that God has the power to come down to our world from time to time and remove people who are causing atrocities - the premise being that if some people were removed from our world, it would be a much better place to live.

Now, because the issue of God's lack of intervention in our world will be addressed more fully later on in this chapter, it will suffice at this point to consider one serious flaw in the proposal that God remove evil people from our world – with whom and where would God begin this process? A difficult question because surely every person is taken with temptation to commit evil, albeit in some sort of lesser form. Indeed, I think it is fair to say that moral evil is a problem which is endemic to society because it occurs in every human to one degree or another. For instance, a child takes another child's toy and causes upset. A person gossips and brings misery to the other person who is spoken about. Someone cheats on their tax return with the result that the government is denied revenue that would help others. Another person crashes their vehicle into a parked car and drives away, leaving the owner to meet the expense of repair.

From these examples, what we see is that if God were to oblige us in our request and remove people who do wrong things from the world, a problem would immediately occur: what degree of evil is acceptable and at what point would we draw the line to determine who is in and who is out? Of course, if it were down to every human being to determine the position of the yardstick by which evil is measured, each person would quite naturally locate the point at which they

Moral Evil

themselves would qualify as being 'not evil'. Indeed, in my years of speaking with people on this subject, I have come across several individuals who truly believe they have never committed an evil act in their life – admittedly, this is their own self-assessment. The implausibility of this aside, it will suffice to observe that moral evil is not so easily determined. One reason is that moral evil requires us to consider it in a more subjective way; it cannot always be calculated or assessed just by the activities that people refrain from.

Within this mix of what is evil is the different issue of the good that people have omitted to do. This is the idea that evil is also the product of our inaction or failure to bring about good in the world – a concept most famously coined in the adapted phrase of political philosopher Edmund Burke who observed 'all that is necessary for evil to triumph is for good men to do nothing[1].' This means that our lack of support towards the unknown person who is starving in the Third World or imprisoned in a dictator state also has consequences for us in terms of evil. So, although a person's intentions may be thoroughly good, there is an argument that their failure to fight for the cause of the needy in the world is tantamount to committing evil, albeit in a different form.

With this in mind, let us now turn our attention from the problem of why God might not oblige our request to visit the world and remove morally evil people to a far greater question that arises from this.

'If God created the world, then why is it so evil?'

It will be helpful to begin this part with an observation that most religious traditions seek to address the problem of evil by determining how to limit its influence in people's lives. By this I mean that most religions recognise evil as a problem which affects individuals and communities alike. Of course, as we have seen, the degree to which humanity is influenced by evil differs from person to person. Factors such as environment, emotional intelligence, and upbringing all seem to play a part in determining how a person matures and the way in which they will engage in or avoid evil activities later on. That said, it also needs be noted that sometimes there is seemingly no explanation for moral evil. For example, a person suddenly commits a random or savage act that is totally out of character with their nature and upbringing. But none of these things comes close to explaining the nature of evil itself and how it is that it exists in our world today.

Now, one problem that people have with the idea of God as a kind, loving heavenly Father who cares for people and is essentially good, is the sense that this is totally at odds with the evil and chaos evident in the world today. And not just in the present day but throughout the centuries and in virtually every part of the world. Indeed, some people even argue that if the world is the product of a good and loving God, there is sufficient reason to challenge the existence of God because evil suggests creation is neither perfect in design or outcome. Similarly, the idea that God maintains control over everything that happens in the world is also problematic in the face of human suffering because a second question arises:

'How could a loving God allow evil to happen in the world?'

Behind this question are two assumptions about the character and nature of God. Firstly, if God is perfectly good (as believers inform us he is) then surely he would not want people to suffer in any way. Secondly, if God is all powerful, he would exercise his power and alleviate or remove suffering from our world.

As already noted, the very presence of evil and suffering in our world has often been seen as calling into question God's integrity and ability to design the world. The logic of such an argument is developed along these lines:

- Suffering exists in the world because of evil actions

- Evil actions imply the world is not perfect but flawed

- As God is the designer of the world, it must be concluded that there must have been some mistake in the construct of the world

- Or that God is capable of both good and evil?

The notion that God is evil or indifferent to human suffering is taken up by Eugene Borowitz, Jewish lecturer, theologian and historian, who concludes that 'Any God who could permit the holocaust, who could remain silent during it, who could hide his face whilst it dragged on ... was [and is] not worth believing in[2].' But this also raises questions about our understanding of what it means for God to be 'perfectly good' and 'perfectly powerful' because implicit in Borowitz's statement are two things:

- Either God wishes to take away evil and is unable to do so – which means God is not omnipotent

- Or God is able to do away with evil but is unwilling – which means God is not really good after all

This line of reasoning was also developed by the 18th century philosopher and historian David Hume, who outlined it this way[3]:

> Is God willing to prevent evil but not able to?
> =>Then he is impotent.
>
> Is he able but not willing?
> =>Then he is malevolent.
>
> Is he both able and willing?
> =>Then where does evil come from?

Moral Evil

It is this question about the origin of evil that has perplexed many people over the centuries. Yet the best explanation of how evil comes to exist independently of God and the world is advanced by Augustine of Hippo who, before converting to Christianity in the fourth century, lived a thoroughly immoral and decadent life – I mention this because I think it will help us to understand the argument that Augustine develops next.

The freewill defence

What Augustine does in his argument is reverse the complaint that is levelled against God by pointing the finger of blame about suffering in the direction of humans who he cites as the arbiters of evil. This argument, known as 'The Freewill Defence[4],' goes something like this:

- For a loving relationship to truly exist between God and creation it is necessary that humans be created in a way that gives each person freedom of choice – allowing them to reject or accept God's advances.

- This necessitates that people are created in a way that does not naturally predispose them towards loving God because this reduces them to little more than robots with a conditioned reflex to love the Divine.

- Instead, for the relationship to be truly meaningful, it requires that God woos humans in a way that is best described as love 'hard won'.

- But here is the rub – in giving humans freedom to choose, God runs the risk that some will reject him.

- Although God may not like this, in order that humans may continue to receive freedom, the Divine is obliged to accept individual choices that go against him.

- As the rejection of God also means a rejection of the Divine essence – namely attributes of goodness and love – it is possible for humans to make choices that run contrary to the good that God desires for humanity. (It is worth noting at this point that humans are unique in this respect as they are able to freely choose in a way that other creatures cannot).

- The consequence of this is that decisions are made which result in good and bad things happening in our world for which we as humans must take personal responsibility.

- Human freewill that is directed away from God explains the reality of unchecked evil as it occurs in the world today.

So the Freewill Defence suggests that evil is a logical necessity if people are enabled to make their own decisions. However, this raises a question in regard to the necessity of freedom over and against the removal of evil.

For instance, a case might be made that people would be happier in a world in which they were programmed to respond to God's loving advances. Especially, if by choosing God in this way, it resulted in a world where people were no longer prone to doing evil. Other benefits of such an arrangement might be that people would experience goodness and harmony between themselves and God with an ability to sense the presence of the Divine in ways that they are currently unable to do. However, although this 'programmed' arrangement might work for a time between God and people, there is also good reason to suppose that humans might eventually come to resent this control over them and their inability to make free and determined choices for themselves. All of which brings us to the dynamics of what constitutes a loving relationship.

In seeking to explain this love dynamic, it will help to begin by clarifying the kind of love that is being discussed here. In his book *The Four Loves* CS Lewis outlines various types of love of which 'agape' [5] is one. Agape is different from the other three because it is unconditional in nature and always directed toward its recipients in selfless ways. This type of love, most commonly associated with the activity of God, usually happens in a way that makes no demand of the receiver to respond or even show gratitude for whatever benefit has occurred. In terms of our discussion, the 'agape' of

God would then be seen as the unconditional love that humanity experiences through the ability to make their own free and determined choices while enjoying the resources of a world that sustains life. Within this there is no requirement that the receivers of this blessing acknowledge God as provider, or any expectation that this gift be accepted or responded to in terms of a relationship with the Creator.

One reason why God acts in this way is best explained in an observation made by the existentialist Jean-Paul Sartre, who notes how the individual 'who wants to be loved does not desire the enslavement of the beloved. He does not want to possess an automaton ... If the beloved is transformed into an automaton, the lover finds himself alone[6].' What this seems to suggest is that the nature of God's love necessitates that freedom must always be the main concern. God allows both outcomes to occur – that is to say that people are free to accept or reject the advances of the Divine even though God knows the consequence when humanity rails against goodness and brings about evil and suffering.

This reluctance of God to overrule our choices poses an interesting question in regard to how the Creator is considered to operate in our world. Many believers hold to the idea that God has the power to overrule our personal freedom by changing our mindset so that we do not pursue a particular course of action. However, this makes little sense and seems unreasonable as it goes against the very nature of God's love that has chosen not to intervene and overrule. Indeed, it might be argued that in the instant that humanity's freewill is taken away from them, God would also be diminished as agape love would no longer exist in the world.

But what does this mean in regard to the world, evil, and suffering? Well, one thing it suggests is that humans occupy a world where God will not always intervene in the way we might imagine. These limitations enable God to remain true to the essence of agape love by not overruling directly in our human affairs, even when these decisions go against the good that God might desire for us.

For example, imagine that I go out to buy some milk from the shop on the corner of my road. As I am leaving the shop, I am spotted by a man who takes an immediate dislike to me. He produces an axe and begins to chase me down the street. Given that the volition of the man is totally bent on seeing me injured, do we suppose that God might overrule the man's mind so that he becomes less disposed to this outcome? No. If this were the case surely no evil would ever occur in the world because God would intervene and stop every instance where it was likely that one person would harm another, and experience tells us this does not happen. Instead, if I am to survive through some intervention of God, it seems more likely that my urgent prayer for fast legs will be answered in such a way that I get away from my assailant or maybe I happen across the path of a police officer who is able to arrest the man.

Now, the important thing to note here is that the axe man's freedom to choose to injure me is not directly usurped by God – by this I mean God does not perform some kind of mind meld on the man encouraging him to think nice thoughts about me. Rather, the man's choice is allowed to occur even though it is evil. The solution that results, in which the axe man is arrested, happens in ways that still allows the man to indulge his desire to chase and injure me. The situation is only countered as the man's will is negated by the intervention of others using their freewill which acts in collective opposition. In this instance my desire and ability to sprint away, or the good fortune of meeting a police officer or others who may overpower the man.

So, in summary, we have looked at some of the problems connected with the issue of moral evil in our world. In this, we have considered how evil could be thought of as a logical outcome if humans are to be enabled to make truly free decisions. The nature of God is not lessened by the outcome of evil in the world, but better understood as evidence of a love that allows things to occur independently of God's nature. With the parameters of moral evil now set in place, let us turn our attention to a different type of evil which is not so easily explained by reference to the action and inaction of individuals – I refer, of course, to the issue of evil that is the outcome of natural disasters in our world.

5 Natural Evil
'Why does God allow natural disasters to occur?'

Like most people, my Christmas festivities came to an abrupt end on 26th December 2004 as I viewed the unbelievable events unfolding in South East Asia. The television images revealed a different side of nature as giant waves rolled onto pleasure resorts and villages, killing thousands of people and leaving a trail of destruction, injury, and despair for those fortunate enough to survive. The horrific carnage of the event left an indelible mark in my mind as I am sure it did in many others.

Quite coincidentally, in the term before the tsunami happened my college studies had been on the issue of human suffering in regard to natural disasters, looking at how theologians throughout the centuries had attempted to explain these events. Although the study material made interesting reading, the tsunami brought the subject back into sharp relief and I found myself reconsidering what I understood and believed about this. Three years on from this disaster I am still thinking through these issues. The only difference is that my thinking has now changed and I ask different questions today from those I asked then.

Now, all that said, I would like to begin by stating right at the start of this chapter that I do not have a complete and wonderful answer on the subject of suffering and natural disasters. Yes, I have a few helpful ideas and some better questions about the subject, but basically the issue is as troublesome for me today as it has always been. In fact, when I present this talk on the Tough Questions Forum I often begin by warning the believers beforehand that what they hear and discuss will be problematic for them because it is not a subject easily defended by those who have faith. My actual words are something like: 'church, we are on an aircraft and we're coming into land, and by the way, there's no undercarriage!'

The reason for issuing a warning is that I am aware how cherished explanations about God and natural disasters held by some believers are easily dismantled by sceptics in the discussion time. My general observation is that most of the orthodox explanations are often simplistic in the assumptions they make about God, and poorly thought out in regard to the contradictions contained within them. Naturally, sceptics do not have the same problem with the reality of natural disasters because they consider these to be purely random events. However, sceptics do have great difficulty with the assertions that believers make in regard to a loving God who is somehow in control of what happens yet chooses not to intervene. This is a position they quite rightly seize upon because they reason that, should a loving God exist, he would not act in such a callous and evil way towards his creation.

Interestingly, explanations from orthodox believers often cite the sovereignty of God and the attributes of the Divine as omniscient, omnipotent and omnipresent

Natural Evil

(all-seeing, all-powerful, and present everywhere). The logic of this argument is that if God has complete control of everything in the universe, then the Divine must also be responsible for events that happen in our world. So when tsunamis, earthquakes, typhoons, hurricanes, storms, floods, landslides or lightening strikes happen, these are considered to have been brought about by God. Indeed, so ingrained is this type of thinking that these events are even referred to as 'acts of God' by some, giving credence to the idea that the Divine has somehow initiated them. If God controls nature, than surely the Divine must somehow influence the natural disasters that happen around the world. And although there are many possible reasons why people might come to think of God as being the arbiter of natural disasters, it seems that this sort of thinking springs from one or more of the following three ideas:

1. Perfect world syndrome
2. Human sinfulness
3. An avenging God

The first two strands are actually interrelated and part of the same idea (taken from the Bible) that humans were introduced into a world that was perfect for them. A world where men and women were encouraged to grow and develop, enjoying an idyllic life. In short, a world where moral and natural evil did not initially exist in any way shape or form. Of course, everything is going well until tragedy strikes – humans transgress the perfect order of the world and chaos and destruction comes into it with the result that the pleasant place is now sullied forever. The consequence is that people are now forced to live in an environment where human relationships are in tatters and the physical environment is affected by natural disasters. The primary reason given for these events happening is that humans have rebelled against God and allowed sin to enter into the world.

The third strand, the idea of an 'avenging God', also relates closely to the other two but centres on the notion that God is rather despotic. God retains control over nature and chooses from time to time to intervene in the world by bringing natural disasters on its inhabitants as part of Divine moral judgements. Of course, it is easy to see how such an idea came into being for it occurs in the Bible. God tells Noah to build an ark because he intends to flood the world and do away with all the evil people. It is a catastrophe in which only Noah's family (through God's intervention) will survive.

Surprising as it will be for some, I do believe that there is scope for the story of Noah to be understood in a different way and with a more plausible explanation as to what might have happened – but that is a whole chapter in a different book! Now, let's shelve this question about Noah for another time and look at each of these strands again, but with a slightly more sceptical eye. I will suggest some different ways of thinking about these ideas and challenge the presumptions often made about our physical world and God's intervention within it. If you are a believer with precious orthodox ideas about the Garden of Eden and how God maintains rigid control of everything, be warned, the plane is coming in to land – there is no undercarriage and it is going to get a bit bumpy.

Perfect world syndrome

This is the idea that humans begin by inhabiting a perfect world; all its features are without fault so that no disease or natural disasters occur to affect the balance of things. But is this a fair assumption to make? After all, the position is problematic given our understanding of the physical world today.

Now, as I will deal with natural disasters more fully in the next section, I will limit the discussion here to how the idea of a perfect world might be currently challenged. In the previous chapter, I looked at the requirement that God places on himself to create a world in which freewill is enabled so that people may choose to accept or reject the Divine. In doing this, God allows people the freedom to engage in activities without fear that he will interfere and usurp their right and ability to choose. This reluctance to intervene also holds true for many other things that affect human activity – take for example gravity.

Let us start by considering gravity as something that God has designed for our benefit. As a community on a planet spinning through space at thousands of miles per hour, I feel confident to speak on behalf of us all and say that we are grateful for the earth's gravity that enables us to live and work and play without fear that one day we will jump too high and be carried off into outer space. We are probably also grateful for the way that gravity benefits us in other ways, allowing us to collect fruit from branches of trees that we might otherwise be unable to reach, or ski down mountains for fun. Indeed, gravity is even part of the hydrological cycle enabling evaporated moisture to return to earth as droplets of rain rather than disappearing upwards into our atmosphere. Gravity has a lot of benefits.

But there is another aspect to gravity that we sometimes fail to consider: in the same way that it facilitates fruit falling from trees, it is also responsible for many other things that may fall on us. So a roof tile may fall off the roof and kill the person standing below because of the gravitational pull that acts on it. Likewise, the same gravity that facilitates a flow of water to the watermill may, on another occasion, result in a flash flood which washes away the mill. Just as gravity keeps people firmly drawn to the earth and allows us to do many things, it may also result in rock slides, avalanches, fallen trees, excessive flooding and other things that are detrimental to human existence. But does the occurrence of such events mean that gravity is a bad thing? Or put another way:

'Would we forfeit gravity rather than run the risk that it might one day cause something detrimental to happen to us?'

Natural Evil

And I am sure that most of us would say that we would not want to do away with gravity (even if that were possible) because we appreciate that the benefits far outweigh any disadvantage that we may encounter from time to time. But what of God in all of this – why doesn't the Divine intervene and save the man who is standing in the spot in which a boulder is about to fall on his head? Well, of course, God could do that. God could intervene whenever a tragedy of gravity was about to occur and save people from a falling object or flash flood. However, in order to achieve this, God might have to intervene in our world in ways and at times that we might not like.

For example, God could intervene and stop people who are working in a stone quarry. The Divine might do this because (with foreknowledge) he knows that their excavation will loosen a boulder that will, at a later date, fall and kill someone. But this might cause hardship for the people who are no longer able to make a living at the quarry because God's intervention brought a stop to the work. Or perhaps God intervenes and stops someone from getting up on the roof of their house to make a repair because the Divine knows the person will fall off and injure themselves. However, later on, this uninjured person might feel aggrieved about this intervention, especially if they are left with a leaky roof and cannot be sure that events would have happened in the way that God said they would.

What we see from these examples is that God does not intervene in this way, for in doing so the Divine would remove from us the capacity to grow, learn and be free in our decision making. It is more than likely that God recognises how our world is full of things that can benefit and harm us. And as difficult as it might be for some of us to accept, it is also quite possible that this is all part of God's intention because for the world to be anything other than this, is to create a sterile environment where people constantly remain subject to the Creator's intervention.

Human sinfulness

This strand centres on the notion that suffering is the product of human activity which came about when people first decided to rebel against God. The result of this is that the world of humans is changed forever. Firstly, the rebellion allows moral evil to come into the world, affecting the way humans relate with one another and with God. Secondly, the delicate balance of the physical world is somehow damaged and the human environment brought into turmoil.

For many, this turmoil is quite clearly recorded in the Bible where the present world is likened to a woman labouring in the pains of childbirth, groaning until physical order can be restored [7]. Now if such a thing is true, it seems to suggest that the extent of sin is more pervasive than humans presently understand because it affects all kinds of environments. But, in the light of scientific understanding, this begs the question of whether such a position can be taken seriously or not.

Natural Evil

Of course, we know from our experience of natural disasters that these may relate to human activity within our world. A good example of this is the extended deforestation of Bangladesh which occurred during the 20th century. The extensive flooding of its plains came about because there were no forested valleys left to absorb excessive rainfall higher up in the mountains. A different example is the 'dust bowl' which occurred when incorrect farming techniques, combined with storms, turned vast areas of the American and Canadian prairie into desert overnight. Perhaps the most common example that people are aware of today is how industrial development has produced greenhouse gases, currently thought to contribute to the climate change that is melting ice caps and raising temperatures around the world.

Now, although all the disasters I have just mentioned are the outcome of human activity in the world, it is questionable whether every phenomenon can be attributed to people in this way. One reason this is problematic is that science now dates the world's existence as millions of years before human life began. Given that there is much evidence to support the claim that earthquakes and tsunamis were happening long before human activity, it is not unreasonable to conclude that natural disasters have their origin in something other than human sinfulness.

This reasoning is reached by an understanding that if the early development of the world required the movement of tectonic plates to create mountains and valleys, then it is equally likely that occurrences of earthquakes, volcanic eruptions and tsunamis began long before humans were ever around to record these events. All of which means that natural disasters simply cannot be the consequence of human rebellion away from God, because these already occurred at a much earlier date in history.

This is most notably advanced in the work of the English naturalist Charles Darwin, who in his attempts to explain how species adapt and develop in their environments, came across Sir Charles Lyell's theory of 'uniformitarianism[8]'. This theory proposed that the world was far older than the date advanced by the Church which had calculated its age by adding together the cumulative years in the genealogy from Adam to Jesus and then an extra 17 centuries after that.

Lyell's theory suggested these biblical calculations were incorrect because the time needed for the weathering and erosion of the landscape to occur (in the rocks he had examined) meant the earth was much older – a planet with an age that should be calculated in millions of years rather than thousands. This theory helped Darwin to begin developing his idea of a gradual sequence of events in the evolution of species and allowed the sciences to advance independently of the Church.

Prior to this, the prevalent view among scholars was that of 'catastrophism', which asserted that the earth had changed as a result of violent cataclysmic events which disrupted the regular order of things within it. What Darwin's model suggested was that change was not sudden but established over lengthy periods of time and in ways that allowed species to adapt and develop in different ways – an idea totally at odds with the global catastrophe described in the Noah account.

So, given that the world and its natural disasters have been in existence far longer than human life and activity, it is not unreasonable to suggest that these phenomena originate from something other than human sinfulness. This brings us to our last strand.

An avenging God

The final strand considers natural disasters from the perspective that they are directed and orchestrated by God. This is the idea that God intervenes and brings about natural disasters to punish human transgression. However, this is immediately problematic as it returns us to the idea that the goodness of God is somehow compromised because the Divine is capable of both good and evil actions. Moreover, it makes God out to be arbitrary because some people are clearly the recipients of these terrible events whereas others are not. The natural disaster makes no discrimination between innocent victim and guilty person.

This indiscriminate destruction of the innocent along with the guilty naturally causes us to question whether it is God who is orchestrating natural disasters. The reasoning being that the Divine would be unlikely to carry out a judgement in such a haphazard and unreliable way. However, during the 18th century, an event happened in Portugal which for many people put the idea of an avenging God finally to rest.

The event happened in the year 1755. It was All Saints' Day and many Christians were at church when the city of Lisbon was rocked by a huge earthquake that lasted approximately 10 minutes. The earthquake caused total devastation, demolishing virtually all of the buildings in the city, killing upwards of 60,000 people and destroying valuable works of art. As the majority of people around that day were believers, this group suffered large in the death toll. Those survivors who managed to escape the earthquake and resulting fire took refuge in Lisbon's less developed sea front area. On the beach people did not run the risk of being struck by falling debris or inhaling smoke, but the choice was not a good one. A short time later, several giant tsunamis swept in from the Atlantic killing the majority of those who had escaped the earthquake.

This event, more than any other, shook the foundations of religious faith within Europe because it challenged the conventional understanding about God in the post-Enlightenment context – an understanding that suggested God was better understood through an examination of the natural world. If this was so, then it seemed God was angry and violent towards creation – moreover, God appeared aggressive towards people and their environments, particularly those who believed and worshipped the Divine.

Natural Evil

In the aftermath of the Lisbon earthquake, many sceptics heaped ridicule on the Church for its unchallenged beliefs about God. French philosopher Francois-Marie Arouet Voltaire, in a poem about the tragedy, wrote:

'This is the result of eternal law
Directing the acts of a free and good God
Did Lisbon, which is no more, have more vices than
London and Paris immersed in their pleasures?
Lisbon is destroyed, and they dance in Paris!' [9]

Voltaire's ridicule of why Lisbon should be singled out by God when other cities in Europe more notoriously decadent were allowed to survive is a reasonable question to ask. A question which deserves better answers than those provided by believers who have sometimes tried to explain these events in terms of the sovereignty of God, or an issue of faith, or as a Divine mystery.

Interestingly, when survivors of the 2004 tsunami were asked to talk about their experience, few of them considered God responsible for the disaster. One possible reason for this could be that we live in a secular age where people do not think such a thing is possible. However, when people were asked a different question about whether God should have intervened, a good number considered that the Divine was powerless to act in such a situation.

From this, it seems that God is no longer seen as the arbiter of the disaster itself but culpable for failing to be powerful enough to intervene. All of which brings us back to what was hinted at in the first strand: whether we like it or not, humans inhabit a world in which nature is savage and as poet Lord Alfred Tennyson describes it: 'red in tooth and claw[10]'. However, on the upside, this is also a world in which people are able to make self-determining choices, enabling them to grow and develop.

Having looked at the three strands, let us next consider three ideas that have been advanced as explanations for how natural disasters might be understood in the world today – two are theological, the other a rational way of thinking about these events.

A spiritual battleground

One theological idea that has been developed in recent years challenges the biblical notion that humans are introduced into a perfect world and suggests instead that our environment was always fractured and prone to natural disasters. This theory is made by theologian Gregory Boyd, who asserts that because evil exists independently of God, there is sufficient reason to consider seriously the biblical explanation that creation is in conflict with spiritual forces that are opposed to God.

In his book *God at War*, Boyd outlines a model in which the origin of evil is explained as happening

Natural Evil

before the creation of humans, brought about by the decision of God to give freewill to all spiritual beings. The result is that some angels use their freedom to oppose God, corrupting themselves into evil beings so that conflict is introduced into the heavenly realms. Later, these 'fallen' angels become an anti-creational force, standing in opposition to God.

The conflict that follows between God and corrupted angels essentially becomes the battle between good and evil. The result of this is that the world sustains damage in such a way that it no longer exists as an idyll because evil is now resident within it. This outcome requires the early biblical narrative to be revised in such a way that it is no longer seen as a creation account but rather, 'God's restoration of a world damaged by a previous conflict which had become formless, futile empty and engulfed by chaos[11].'

The restoration theory advanced by Boyd develops the idea that 'the earth is birthed, as it were in an infected incubator [because] it is fashioned in a warfare context [being] altogether good, but made and preserved over and against forces that are perpetually hostile to it[12].' A context in which humans, as God's agents, are later called upon to conquer an evil being who has invaded creation. So Boyd sees human suffering as an inevitable consequence of a spiritual battle that is currently taking place and earth and its inhabitants are located in the midst of this conflict.

Wrong place – wrong time

This response is not really a theological one as much as it is a reasoned position that questions the way in which humans respond to the effects of natural disasters. Although many natural disasters make headline news because they result in death and destruction, it is important to remember that natural phenomena often occur in places that are sparsely populated and in ways that do not result in loss of human life. Interestingly, when these events occur in places where people are not affected directly, human complaint is conspicuously quiet. This suggests that what qualifies as a natural disaster is dependent on whether it has caused damage to human existence.

So for example, a tropical storm or tsunami that destroys an area of coral reef but does no harm to human life or industry is unlikely to be seen in ways that would render it an evil event – even though the destruction of the reef might result in the extinction of many rare species of coral and animal life.

Now, let us imagine that it is a thousand years on. People come and settle in the place where the coral reef once was because it is picturesque and has potential as a place for tourism. The fact that it is an area at risk of flooding from a tsunami is not considered. After all, as far as people are aware, it has never been prone to these disasters before. Of course, when a tsunami happens years later, this time killing people now living in the area, the cry is one of an unfair world or uncaring God when really the decision to populate risky areas rested with human decision making. Had the reef area been considered dangerous and left unpopulated there would be no loss of human life when the tsunami occurred again years later. Likewise, there would be no need to accuse God about his wantonness in creating such a dangerous world for people to inhabit.

Humans throughout the centuries have often populated areas which have been considered unsafe in terms of natural disasters. Indeed these places are frequently considered as accidents waiting to happen and yet development continues – suggesting that human need of an area may outstrip any concern people might have about a disaster occurring. Some of the more obvious places are populated areas that have suffered a previous disaster and have since redeveloped. Examples of this are settlements along the San Andreas fault-line and the development of Lisbon and Tokyo, two cities that have experienced earthquakes in the past.

Although many people choose to ignore the possible outcomes of living in an unsafe area for reason of lifestyle choice – by this I mean that they choose to live there because of its beautiful scenery or future economic prospects – it must be noted that not all people have such choice. I refer here to those who are disadvantaged in ways that make them unable to choose where they live. The economically poor have no choice about living along a fault line, or in an area that is liable to flooding, or in the shadow of a volcano. All of which suggests it is an unfair assumption that because people are located in a potential disaster zone, this is always through their own choice.

In summary 'Wrong place, wrong time' deals with the reasonableness of human responses to natural disasters as they occur, particularly in regard to people's failure to recognise that it is often a series of human decisions that have led communities to develop in a place that is liable to destruction. The argument is that should the choice be made differently and people live in areas that are reasonably safe from natural disasters, the likelihood of death from these events would be greatly reduced. However, such choices are not always practical in our world, where space and economic resources are often limited.

The world that God designed

This last idea is a theological one and is taken from the concluding part of a television programme called *'Tsunami – Where was God?'* [13] which was broadcast in December 2005, a year after the South East Asia disaster.

In this programme, the interviewer Mark Dowd finishes his travels by journeying to Vatican City to attend a conference of Jesuit physicists who are meeting to discuss climate change. Seeking an opportunity to ask them questions about how they would each reconcile a world of natural disasters with the idea of a loving God, the interviewer is surprised by the fact that none of the physicists share his dilemma. The physicists explain the necessity of tectonic movement in the world as part of the process by which they understand how human life is enabled to develop and be maintained. Their answers arrived at through the consideration of what the world would be like if earthquakes and volcanic eruptions were not an integral part of its development – a world totally unsuited to sustaining human life.

To summarise, this last idea considers the possibility that our world, affected as it is by natural disasters, is also the environment that is best suited to propagating human life. Our world is not safe from these types of phenomena yet supports life by the very fact that these natural events exist. Basically this is a world that is best described as 'red in tooth and claw,'[10] where humans may grow and develop, yet there is always the risk that life might be removed in an instant.

6 Death and Illness
'Why did my friend have to die?'

Without a doubt this will be a difficult chapter to write for several reasons. The first reason is that this is a completely new topic for me because it is not one of the original sessions from the Tough Questions Forum. Although a lot of the ideas I am using have not been previously used within the context of a discussion setting, a good deal of the material has been informed by my conversations with people over the years who have been seeking answers to difficult events that have happened in their lives. More often, these tragedies have caused them to rethink what they understand and believe about God in the light of their experience.

A second reason that I think this chapter will be difficult to write is that I am aware that the subject is an emotive issue for many people because they will come to the material having already experienced some kind of bereavement or loss in their lives. Not unusually, the occurrence of this tends to increase with age as people around us – friends, colleagues, family members and relatives – suffer illness or die. The deep hurt that is experienced during these times happens because the person was close to us and has now been taken out of our sphere of relationships.

Other times, the hurt may relate to a different kind of separation, such as when someone we know develops a debilitating illness. For example, dementia, and is incapacitated and/or no longer remembers us. The bottom line in all of this is that the disappointment of losing our close friend, colleague, or family member – in whatever manner – can be absolutely devastating. Moreover, there are no words or answers that can truly comfort us when these things happen. It is as if we are overcome by a cloud of darkness because we no longer have that person to talk and share our life with. Indeed, no amount of kind words will ever make it right.

Lastly, I am aware of how my own life has been affected by the illness and death of people around me. As an ordained minister who regularly visits the sick and conducts a fair number of funerals each year, I am very aware of how the dying process affects people – those who suffer a terminal illness and those who are left to grieve.

In my own life I have experienced bereavement a number of times, the most recent being the loss of my parents, both to lung cancer. My mother's death was a slow and painful process as her health deteriorated over a period of months. The disturbing sight of her at the local hospital anchored to an oxygen tank and unable to breathe is a sad memory that will remain with me forever. The other abiding memory from this time was the sense of complete helplessness I felt each evening as I said goodbye to my mother, uncertain that I would see her again when I returned the following day.

Reflecting on these experiences over the years, it is my observation that this type of pain never leaves the individual completely but rather just becomes more manageable with the passing of time. However, I am also aware that sometimes even the slow process of recovery for the bereaved can be derailed, especially when death is inadequately resolved due to questions remaining over what actually happened – as when some mystery is connected with the death because the body is never found, or a third party was involved in the incident, or a coroner's report or inquiry is necessary. The relative or friends' desire for an adequate resolution of the matter often hinders their ability to grieve, with the result that they may remain bitter for the remainder of their lives.

Interestingly, when a third party is eventually convicted, it does not always bring the comfort to the family or friends in the way they might have hoped for. The comments made by grieving family members outside courtrooms only seems to confirm how ineffective the judicial process often is in reducing the pain that people may be experiencing.

Now, in the same way that the bereaved are sometimes derailed by a third party, I think the same principle may also apply where people take offence at God for what has happened to a loved one. We saw something of this in the preceding chapters where people came to consider God culpable for evil and suffering, possibly because their grief came about through an event in which someone was murdered or killed or maimed. And hopefully, from what was developed in those chapters, we may now begin to look at these issues with a slightly different mindset. But in regard to the issue of illness in our world, which cannot be adequately explained by human activity or the movement of the tectonic plates, people quite reasonably ask:

'If God created the world so perfect, why is there so much disease and illness within it?'

It is necessary to state here that this question is not without a theological explanation. Many orthodox believers consider disease and illness to have come about as a result of human rebellion from God. This is the idea that when humans rejected God and became prone to moral evil, so the world, which was under their stewardship, also became affected. The result of this was a defiled world in which the once-perfect idyll was lost for ever – or at least until humanity can be restored back to God at the end of time.

The difficulty with this sort of orthodox explanation is that others find the idea unsatisfactory in terms of the actions of a loving God. Indeed, some people actually reason that if God is all-seeing and all-knowing and knew how humans would fail and allow illness and death to enter into the world, the Divine must also be considered responsible. After all, God gave humans the task in the first place and must have known the irreparable damage they would cause to their environment through their error.

Naturally, sceptics adopt a different approach by reasoning that it is nonsense to think that the physical world might be designed in such a way as to be affected by human decisions. Whereas human activities may result in changes to the environment, this is a long way removed from orthodox ideas of how the world is affected by a spiritual reality that has introduced illness and death into it. True, human decisions do have outcomes for people in the world, like when rich nations prosper at the expense of the poor, but this begs another question:

'Can our decisions really be seen as responsible for disease and illness in the world?'

Clearly there is a sense in which human decisions may affect health in a very direct way. We see this most obviously in the lifestyle choices that people make where the risk of illness is increased through consumables such as alcohol, cigarettes, or fatty foods. Sometimes the dangers of these products are known to the individual beforehand though a decision is made to continue with it, usually because it is enjoyable. These lifestyle decisions are particular to each person and the way they exercise their own freewill – we can choose to live healthy or unhealthy lives, for instance, eating bacon sandwiches for breakfast or cereal.

Of course, decisions can affect us in less obvious ways, such as when the consequence of what we have done is not apparent to us. A good example of this is the issue of passive smoking, where the inhalation of another person's second-hand smoke is now recognised as dangerous. This danger was only discovered after millions of people had been exposed to it for many years. Although the danger of active and passive smoking is now obvious to us, risks associated with other products and activities are less apparent. I am thinking here of products that people have used for a number of years but which are only later recognised as detrimental to health because they contain materials which are cancerous or harmful.

A good example of this is asbestos which was manufactured and used in the building industry for much of the last century. In fact, the use of this material dates back to 4,000 BC when it was added into wicks by people to increase the length of time that lamps and candles were able to burn. In Ancient Egypt, the material was woven into fabric to make cloth that was used to prepare pharaohs for burial. Indeed, even Benjamin Franklin is known to have brought a purse made from asbestos to England in the 19th century. However, in recent times it has become evident that the dust particles from asbestos has resulted in many people developing lung and respiratory problems as they unwittingly absorbed it into their bodies.

Similarly, foodstuffs and skin products are often withdrawn from stores when it has been discovered that the things used to enhance or preserve them have been detrimental to health. Indeed, even as I write, researchers are issuing a warning regarding the consumption of processed meat (ham, salami, bacon) which they believe may lead to the development of cancer. So, having considered how human activity may result in disease and illness, let's advance the question further and ask:

'What about death and illness that cannot be explained by reference to humans 'meddling' with their environment?'

Many diseases and illnesses have occurred in our history in ways and at times when there was no obvious link to human activity or interference. My intention for the remainder of this chapter is to provide some instances by which we might reason why illness might be a necessary part of the world we inhabit.

Clearly, there are strains of illness that repeat themselves over time. An example of this is influenza – a viral infection that has the capacity to adapt and develop into more virulent strains. Although the recurrence of these viruses can be quite frequent, they may also occur in more haphazard ways, by which they develop and become pandemics.

This is a major concern for governments around the world who are currently aware of the risk carried by bird flu which has accounted for millions of deaths over the years. A characteristic of the bird flu virus is the way it develops in other creatures first and only passes to humans at a much later stage – sometimes in ways that may skip several generations. From this, it is apparent that humans cannot be held responsible for the way the virus develops other than that they are its unwitting recipients and hosts, carrying it from one person to the next. This aspect of how infections are passed between people leads us onto our next aspect – the human immune system.

While it is apparent that the immune system of a human is generally robust in dealing with infections, it is clear that there are periods in the human lifecycle when the body is less able to manage these events. Two such times are: infancy when the body is learning to fight infection, and old age when the body is not so strong. Another time when the human defence might fail is when a new virus is encountered which the immune system has no experience of and is insufficiently equipped to deal with.

A classic example of this occurred in New Zealand in the late 18th century with the arrival of colonists from Great Britain, who unwittingly introduced the indigenous Maori population to a range of infectious illnesses. These viruses, such as chicken pox, measles and the common cold, had never been encountered by the Maoris and many were unable to fight these new infections. A sizeable proportion of the indigenous population died within a decade.

Nowadays, humans have developed antibiotics to assist the immune system in helping people fight infection. However, although penicillin and other antibiotics have saved many lives, present day medicine advises against the repeated use of these

Death and Illness

drugs for fear they will inadvertently weaken the immune system. The problem is that the virus, also a living thing, desires to survive and so adapts to these new antibiotics creating even more complex infections – infections that may later go beyond the capacity of the human immune system. Of course, a different problem that arises from this is the failure of humanity to keep pace with these viruses, which continually require new antibiotics to be developed and manufactured.

Research into the causes of illness over the years has not only helped people to identify and understand diseases better but has also resulted in a large number of cures being developed. A good example of this relates to leprosy, an infection which, when left untreated, affects the person's nerves, causing damage to skin, limbs and eyes. Although the Bible and other documents record that people had leprosy in times that predate Jesus Christ, it was not until the end of the last century that the bacteria that caused this condition was discovered. Previous to this, many people considered leprosy incurable and managed it by keeping the infected individual separate from everyone else. However, the discovery by the Norwegian physician Gerhard Hansen that the disease was caused by a particular bacterium (*Mycobacterium leprae*) was later advanced by others who developed multidrug treatments to cure individuals with leprosy.

Although scientific discoveries in the future are likely to result in more cures becoming available, it is important we consider a different issue about the nature of these constructs within our world. We encountered this in the previous chapter when looking at the advantages and disadvantages of gravity. In this, we considered how the benefits of gravity will always far outweigh the disadvantages. Similarly, the same line of thinking might also be applied to our understanding of bacteria. For instance, our current understanding about how different bacteria operate and affect human health (often in quite positive ways) might cause us to rethink whether we would truly want to live in a world which was devoid of bacteria. We might even ask the question whether bacteria are not part of the way that God has designed this world to operate.

Again, similar questions arise in regard to the issue of human genetics, which has received much attention in recent years. The research, developed from earlier findings of DNA, suggested that the survival of each species is dependent on genetic anomalies that enable them to adapt to new or changing environments. So, in a barren area, the giraffe with a longer neck who can reach the highest foliage that hangs from a tree is more likely to survive than giraffes with shorter necks. As our tall giraffe mates with another tall-necked giraffe, the resulting offspring carry the parents' DNA and the likelihood of producing tall offspring is greatly increased.

This observation that species develop independently (and often at the expense of others) has led to ideas about a specific type of 'gene' existing within the DNA of every surviving species. The suggestion is that this gene selfishly seeks its own genetic construct to be advanced at expense of everything else. From this, it is easy to see the dilemma that might face the Divine in designing a world in which living things are given opportunity to develop. If God creates a world that is too tight in its structure, it is possible that human life might not develop. However, if God creates the earth in a less deterministic way there runs the contrary risk that this will encourage a variety of other things to develop in ways that will allow disease and illness to occur – a world in which humans may flourish along with giraffes, bacteria and other viruses.

So in summary, if God makes the world too precisely, then the Divine runs the risk that life might not emerge. But, if God loosens up control of the world so that life can emerge, there is a risk that other things will also develop which might compete with humans for life. All of which begs the question:

'Isn't God bothered by human death and dying?'

The 'Bigger Picture'

Perhaps the thing that bothers people most about suffering today is the sense of waste or futility when people die as a result of illness, evil actions or natural disasters. Central to these concerns is a sense that the life of the deceased individual has somehow been cut short or left unfulfilled. But this is largely a secular perspective on life because its assumption is that the time we live on earth is the only time available to us. A position which is contrary to spiritual perspectives which understand it in terms of:

Life => death => afterlife

Imagine a scene outside someone's house. A person is watching a caterpillar move along a branch. As the person observes the caterpillar, they notice that it slows to a stop. A few days later, the person returns to the place where the caterpillar was and sees that it is now a lifeless indistinguishable object on a branch. Around the body a hard layer of shell has formed, disfiguring the caterpillar's shape. Outraged at this outcome, the person speaks out angrily at the unfairness of life and the cruelty of a God who would create an insect that was so limited, only to bring it to such an ignominious end. The person's rant complete, they enter the house and think no more of it.

A few days later, as the person walks along the path close by the tree, they notice that something unexpected has begun to happen. The chrysalis shell that has formed around the lifeless body of the caterpillar now has a hole in it. The person stops and watches and sees the shell being discarded by a beautiful butterfly. As they watch, the butterfly eventually spreads its wings and flies away as its metamorphosis is now complete.

Later on, as the person reflects on the events they have witnessed, they are forced to consider how the caterpillar has been liberated in a way they could not have initially imagined. The person now begins to rethink whether what they once considered tragedy was instead a transitory stage to a different life. The observer notes how the butterfly's departure from the branch displays a far greater range of movement and beauty than it ever had before.

The believers' understanding that death is a stage or transition point by which people transfer from this world into the next challenges the ideas that some people have concerning the necessity for longevity of physical life. Indeed, it might even be argued that if a future life (the other side of death) brings release for people from pain and suffering, then death is not necessarily the bad thing that people might suppose it to be. Rather, it might be considered as a stage people pass through carrying a degree of fear because death is the great unknown and not necessarily the end of life per se.

So could it possibly be that God has a larger plan – one that does not consider death in the same way that humans view it, but sees it rather as a stage or transit point from the physical world into the spiritual realm? If this is so, then death is no longer a tragedy but a positive. Interestingly, this is something that might also provide hope and comfort to people in their grief.

Consider next, a different kind of turmoil as we look at the issue of world religions and the dilemma of what truth to believe.

The God of the Cruel World

7 World Religions
'Do all religions lead to God?'

Let me begin this chapter by noting that there are not enough pages in this book to consider all the religions of the world and the way they seek to answer this question. Peculiar to most religions is the respective claims they make about how the revealed truth of God will only be found within their group and understanding. Now, because religious groups compete with one another to get people to respond to their particular message, many people would like to know which truth about God is actually correct. The hope is that if the one and only true religion was known, it would enable the false claims of everyone else to be dismissed. However, here begins the problem.

In the quest for understanding whose revealed truth to believe, people have become aware of how religions differ from one another, both in terms of their understanding of God and the rites of passage they require. Indeed, for the believer to commit to one religious group usually means that they cannot be, at the same time, practising within another.

This is the nature of religious expression because each one creates its own mutually exclusive group. But as people take time to explore these religions and understand the different complexities, so they also come to realise that there is something more at stake. The revealed truth about God usually contains within it a directive to humans as to how they will transit from this world into the next life – a transit that requires people to believe and respond to the claims of one particular religion. For those who do not avail themselves of the opportunity to escape to a different world, the outcome is usually negative, involving punishment and alienation from God. This is quite problematic for the 'would be' believer, who is faced with the choice of which religious truth to accept because to choose wrongly is to run the risk of suffering an eternal consequence. So returning to the question:

'Do all religions lead to God?'

We begin to understand why many people become confused and nervous about who and what they should believe in. For others, the variety of religions and the multitude of truths, lead them to the contrary idea that all groups must access the same God. However, common to both approaches is the notion that this is a significant question to ask. In fact, it is not a single question but an amalgamation of several questions that seek answers to the following:

- **If God exists, is there a specific requirement as to how I should understand and respond to this?**

- **Why would God choose to be revealed by one religion and not others?**

- **What are the consequences if I choose a way that does not lead to God?**

- **How can anyone believe such nonsense? (the atheist's question)**

Now it will be useful to say that what is advanced in the following pages has been developed from a model by Reverend Alan Race[14] who attempts to explain the issue of different religions from within a Christian perspective. His explanation references three possible positions that people might have – pluralist, exclusivist, or inclusivist. I will outline and explain these positions, contrasting the different perspectives of each to show the strengths and weaknesses within these models.

Pluralism

Quite simply, the pluralist believes that God is to be discovered in every one of the world religions. This is the idea that no one religion has a monopoly about what truth is nor possesses the only way to access God. Rather, each has a partial understanding of God – an understanding that is incomplete without being added together to form a collective truth with all other religious groups.

The pluralist believes that people from different religions worship the same God but just do not understand that this is what is happening. The revealed truth of each religion is no greater than that of another because all have equal value. And as pluralism is more of a theory than a revealed truth – because there is no religious leader associated with it – its ideas have often been explained through illustrations such as the 'blind scribes' and 'routes up a mountain' which we shall consider next.

The blind scribes

This illustration requires people to imagine a scenario in which religious leaders from each of the major religions find themselves together in a room. Each leader is blindfolded and led outside to an elephant. The leader is then placed at a strategic point beside the elephant and asked to feel what is in front of them and describe it.

- The Jew who feels the elephant's ear describes it as 'a large leathery curtain'
- The Hindu feels the tail and describes it as 'like rope'
- The Muslim puts his arms around the leg and says it feels like 'a tree trunk'
- The Christian feels the elephant's trunk and says it feels like 'a hose or large water pipe'

The pluralist explanation of this illustration is that in the same way the blind scribes are unable to define the 'whole' elephant, so too, this is what happens in the major world religions. Each of the religious leaders such as Moses, Jesus, Mohammad, and Guru Nanak, attempt to explain God while not in possession of all the information – or elephant in this case. The pluralist argues that should the blindfold be removed from each of these leaders, they would see how they are all describing the same God, just from different positions.

Routes up a mountain

This approach is similar to the first but seeks to explain how people from different religions are all on the same journey to God. The major religions are located at different positions around the base of a mountain and are unable to view one another as they ascend from the north, south, east and west. As each group makes its way towards the summit, they do not see others who are also climbing from different positions – the view of each is obscured by the rock face in front of them. As they climb higher, they are only able to see the ground below where their base camp is.

From this, the pluralist asserts that all religious groups are actually on the same journey to God, just by different routes. If the religious leaders were able to see the mountain from a position above the summit, they would realise how all of these routes converge on the same point. In other words, people are making different journeys but the reality is that they will all one day arrive at the same destination. For many people, this idea is quite compelling as it appeals to modern society's desire for balance and political correctness because it:

- makes few intellectual demands on the believer.
- accepts all religions as equally true and valid.

- has a morally superior air of tolerance and acceptance of all people

However, at the risk of disappointing some who think the pluralist argument is a convincing one, there are some major flaws within it which we will look at now.

The first problem occurs in the illustration of the 'blind scribes'. The pluralist argument is that if only the religious leaders were able to see, they would understand the truth of God. But this is a truth which only the pluralist narrator is capable of knowing, which raises questions in regard to what other presumptions have been made within the illustration.

With reflection, what we see is that the pluralist narrator also deals in revealed truth. However, unlike the religious leaders who are considered misdirected in their ideas and thinking, the pluralist is the only one who sees things clearly and recognises the elephant for what it is. And although this initially sounds reasonable, what we come to realise is that this claim is more outrageous than those made by the religious leaders. For only the pluralist is able to see everything perfectly in the same way that God might. Basically, the narrator claims to have a greater understanding and insight than the collective thought of Moses, Jesus, Mohammad, or any of the other religious teachers for that matter.

Similarly, the illustration of 'routes up the mountain' is also problematic. The pluralist assumes that s/he has a position above the summit and is able to see what others cannot. Again, the implication is that the narrator has parity with God for only s/he can see the one truth from the many. Of course, these illustrations are flawed in other ways because not all routes might reach the mountain summit. Likewise, one of the scribes might actually identify the elephant correctly for what it is rather than what it's not.

However, what is far more compelling are the conflicting claims that different religions make in regard to one another which suggest that spiritual routes do not converge in the way that the pluralist might think. Cultural differences aside, the suggestion that every religion ultimately has the same message and that believers achieve the same spiritual end point is something most groups would differ on. One reason we know this is because faith groups often make competing claims as to what is truth, usually in ways that contradict what other religions state and believe. This is clearly evident in the claims made about Jesus by Islam and Christianity, namely that Muslims consider him a prophet and Christians believe him to be God incarnate.

Indeed, from our earliest years we become aware of a specific order that means one person's engagement with a particular religion necessitates that they must be devoted to it at the expense of all other possibilities. For instance, being a Jew and a practising Muslim are mutually incompatible in terms of the rites of passage they require, but also in the way that worship is conducted. This alone illustrates how ludicrous the suggestion is that all religions are in essence the same, and does not even begin to touch upon those whose truth claims require the destruction of other faith groups that are different to themselves. Consider next the idea of Christian exclusivism.

Exclusivism

There are many religions that make exclusivist claims. By this I mean groups who assert that their religion or thinking is true and that everything outside of it is incorrect or invalid. These sorts of claims are made by Islam, Judaism, Christianity and others, where each group believes that they have a revealed truth about God that others do not have. And of course, we might also add to this list atheism, even though it would not define itself as a religion, because its own particular creed is that 'God does not exist'.

Of course, Christian exclusivism asserts that God does exist and that the only way the Divine may be fully understood and accessed is through Jesus Christ. As a result, the believer's knowledge and experience of God is mediated exclusively through Christ in ways that affirm this belief – a belief which necessitates that other religions be considered as false attempts to reach/worship God.

Now, although this position is the mainstay of exclusivist belief, the idea of other groups being false attempts to access God was not initially formulated with world religions in mind. One reason we know this is that most of these 'other' religions were unknown to the church at the time when Christian doctrine was first developed – the boundary of Christianity going no further than the limits of the Roman Empire. Limits that knew nothing of places such as India, Australia, and Brazil, let alone the religious practices of the people within these countries.

From church history it seems that the instructions towards people with 'false' ideas relate more to the growth of religious 'sects' within the Church itself. These groups threatened the orthodox position through their contrary ideas regarding the person and divinity of Jesus Christ. Eventually, as these heresies became more widespread, the early Church Fathers chose to identify and isolate these 'sects' within the Church. Of course, this is not to suggest that the exclusivist position accommodates other faiths, for clearly it does not. However, it does help us to understand how the church has come to hold both exclusivist and inclusivist ways of thinking. The exclusivist approach centres on how people are given freewill and have the choice to respond to or reject the message of Christ. Where people have no knowledge of Jesus to inform this choice, the belief is that individuals are judged by God on the basis of how they responded to the general revelation of the Divine as it was mediated to them through:

- Nature – the evidence of creation itself
- Human conscience – a belief in the existence of a Divine Being

Naturally, the problem that many people have with exclusivism is they consider it arrogant because of the claims made by its followers in regard to it being the one and only truth, and that all other religions are wrong. This position is equally problematic because we live in an age where to make such a claim is to be considered divisive. Central to people's discomfort with exclusivist claims are two main issues:

1. **The idea that God might choose only one way to reveal himself**

2. **A sense of unfairness that God would only accept this route for people to be forgiven and restored**

Although each of these issues sounds feasible in terms of human reasoning and sensibility, it needs to be noted that we are not dealing with a human response here but the character and nature of God. In other words, if God is going to be God, and not something that humans can manipulate into doing what they want, it is not unreasonable to expect that the Divine might have only one way by which people might know truth and find salvation. For it to be anything else is for humans to reduce God to what they would like the Divine to be. Indeed, the anomaly of whether it is fair or unfair does not even come into it, because such an idea presumes that God can be defined and affected by our limited human understanding of what is good and right.

So, in summary, the exclusivist believes that God has been revealed in one way only and that other religions are mistaken in their belief that they may access the Divine by their own particular rites of passage. The Christian exclusivist's belief is that it is only through Jesus Christ's death on a cross and a person's willingness to respond to this that people are made right with God and enabled to access eternal life. With the exclusivist position outlined, consider next the contrasting and challenging idea of inclusivism.

Inclusivism

Like the pluralist, the Christian inclusivist also believes that God is made known through each of the world religions. However, the inclusivist believes that full and complete knowledge of the Divine can only be gained through Jesus Christ. Now to understand the dynamics of the inclusivist approach, it is necessary to journey back to the 1960s and the Second Vatican Council (of the Roman Catholic Church) which wrestled with the issues of how people from other faiths should be considered in terms of Christ's salvation. The conclusion of 'Vatican 2' was that while its members believed that everlasting salvation could only be found through faith in Jesus Christ, special provision should be extended to those people from other traditions who:

> 'through no fault of their own do not know the gospel of Christ or his Church, yet sincerely seek God and, moved by grace, strive by their deeds to do [God's] will as it is known to them through the dictates of conscience[15].'

In reaching this decision, the council also recognised and affirmed that whatever was true and holy in other faiths also reflected 'a ray of that truth which enlightens all men[15]'. Central to this line of thinking was the idea that other religions should be thought of as at a stage of being 'pre-Christian' rather than 'non-Christian' as the council believed that each one was ordained to find its fulfilment in Christ.

Of course, the inclusivist approach differs from pluralist ideas in that it does not suggest that all religions lead to God but rather that although other religions may display something of the truth of the Divine, the complete truth comes only through Jesus Christ. The suggestion of the Second Vatican Council was that other religions may also be considered participants in this process because Christ secures the possibility of eternal salvation for all people through his death and resurrection, irrespective of how they came to believe in him. The idea developed by Council members proposes that Christ's salvation is granted to people in one of two ways – the

- Ordinary way of salvation
- Extraordinary way of salvation. [15]

'Ordinary' salvation

This type of salvation is considered to exist for people from other faith groups who have not heard the gospel of Christ but have worshipped the Divine within the religion they were brought up in. Had these people been born at a different time or in a different context, where there was opportunity to learn about Jesus, the likelihood is that they would have become followers of Christ. The thinking behind this is that although Jesus makes limited reference to people from other religions in the Bible, there is sufficient reason to presume that his sacrifice extends to others who do not profess to know him. Certainly the Bible details many people who received help from Jesus even though they were not Jewish. The argument is that in the same way that Jesus is prepared to help these people while they are alive, so the likelihood is the same generosity will extend to them later on at the point of death.

The notion that people are saved by the sacrifice of Jesus, and not by their worship and rites of religion, is not a new idea within the Church. However, in regard to people from other faiths, the idea becomes quite problematic because it implies that these other attempts to worship God are somehow less than those which occur in the Christian experience. However, it is worth noting that the term 'ordinary' salvation seems to suggest an experience which is commonplace to the majority of people who do not recognise or understand Jesus as their saviour during their physical lifetime.

'Extraordinary' salvation

The 'extraordinary' way of salvation refers to people who have come to see and understand Jesus as their saviour during their lifetime. The experience of God's revelation leads the individual to become a follower before physical death occurs. The result of this is that salvation is understood early on in the believer's life in ways that are considered 'extraordinary' because it seems to have been revealed directly to the individual by God.

Criticism of inclusivism

With inclusivism defined, let us turn our attention to the major criticism that is levelled against it. Interestingly, it is a criticism that comes from within the Church itself for it is Christian exclusivists who have the greatest problem with inclusivity. The exclusivist argues that accommodation of these faith groups (without placing a requirement on people to change and respond to Christ) is contrary to what Jesus teaches about there only being one way to God. Exclusivists fearing that this openness towards people from other religions moves the Church closer to pluralist and universal ways of thinking – a route which might also, in the process, dilute the message of Christ.

A different argument against inclusivity centres on Jesus' instructions to his followers to make disciples of all nations. Here, the exclusivist reasons that if people from other religions can be saved without making a response to Christ, the need to tell others about Jesus becomes redundant. Moreover, it raises questions about what Jesus' intention might have been in telling the disciples to go and do this if he knew people could be saved in other ways which did not require explicit faith in Jesus Christ.

So, in summary, the inclusivist perspective considers that other religions do reveal some truth about God, but that the complete truth is found only in the person and work of Jesus Christ. People from other faiths are saved not by their own religion but through salvation that is secured through Christ. In short, people of other faiths access God's salvation via Jesus Christ BUT not always through explicit faith in Him.

Now let us turn our attention to human attempts to explain the way in which God is considered absent or 'missing' from our world.

8 Invisible God
(Is it possible to prove God's existence?)

In the early days of the Tough Questions Forum, when most of the talks were still unwritten, the team shared out the topics for discussion between one another. Initially there were just three talks so we shared them three ways. A friend volunteered to do the talk on whether it was possible to prove God's existence. As the time came near for his presentation to be given, I asked him how the talk was progressing and what angle he intended looking at it from. Although his answer worried me slightly, he told me he would be tackling the question with reference to the design argument – it was not until the night of the talk that we realised the mistake he had made.

His outline, which was reasonably well put together, centred on the idea that God's existence could be proven through reference to the intricacies of design found in the world. On the night of the talk, the audience of sceptics and believers generously listened to his presentation – the sceptics listening more in a sort of stunned silence than anything else! The presentation concluded and the people moved into their groups to discuss what they had just heard.

Now, if I had any doubt that my friend's talk had not met its objective of arguing for the existence of God, this was confirmed by what occurred in the next 45 minutes. Sceptics (and even some believers) rounded on the naivety of his argument, challenging it in all manner of ways in every one of the three discussion groups. Indeed, even I struggled with what had been said as I was aware how sceptics would disagree with the premise that because something exists, it implies someone designed it.

Of course, this presentation happened a few years ago now and I have had more time to think through this question and prepare a different argument from the one that was given on that night. This question has probably caused more debate over the centuries than any other question, the issue of whether God exists or not. Or rather, put another way –

'Is it possible for humans to prove God's existence in a consistent way that will convince others of this reality?'

In addressing this question, I think it is fair to begin with an observation that although many theologians have set out to establish the likelihood of a Creator, none of them have ever been truly successful in this endeavour. By that I mean that no theologian or philosopher has ever advanced an argument or formula concerning God that proves the existence of the Divine beyond all reasonable doubt. These arguments are usually well constructed and cover a number of areas such as

- The ontology of God (God exists as perfect being)
- How the mechanisms of the world point to a designer

- The cosmos
- Miracles (as evidence of a higher power)
- Morality

That said, none of these arguments offers a really watertight proof of God's existence. True, the explanations that have been developed at different periods in history have often been convincing for a time, but no one has ever provided conclusive evidence that God exists. At best, an idea is advanced which makes an appeal to the 'approximate God' – arguing over the probability that God is more likely to exist than to not exist. Of course, this lends itself to a sort of 'guess estimate' about God where people piece together as much of the jigsaw as they can and then imagine God within the gaps that are left.

Hopefully, no one will think me unfair in making this observation because I believe it is an honest assessment of how people have sought to prove and understand God's existence in the world. Indeed, the very requirement that people exercise 'faith' seems to necessitate that believers are required to place their trust in something that is presently unverifiable. And of course, if we could verify God as a definite fact, there would be little need for faith – people would make their assessment based on solid evidence. So, returning to the question:

'Is it possible to prove God's existence?'

I would like to give a bold answer and say a resounding **'NO'**, because I do not believe it is possible for humans to prove God's existence. However, I would also like to say that whereas humans may not be able to prove God's existence, this does not mean that God is unverifiable. Should we rearrange the question and ask:

'Is it possible for God to prove his existence to us?'

I think the answer is a resounding **'YES'**. God is quite capable of proving his existence to us if God wants to. Yet the Divine does not do this, which begs a different question altogether:

'Why might God not be revealed?'

And it is this question that I will attempt to address in the following pages. Of course, both atheist and believer have stock responses to this question. The believer states that God has been revealed through creation but humanity fails to comprehend this. The atheist reasons in the opposite direction that God cannot be revealed because God does not exist.

Now, although these two positions mark out each end of the faith spectrum, they unfortunately also polarise thought into one of two camps – people who believe in God and those who do not. With these positions identified, what I will do next is steer a 'middle course' between the two by considering a question that I have seldom heard discussed:

'Why might God be hidden from humanity?'

Interestingly, this approach addresses sceptical concerns about the absence of evidence for God while also giving scope to the possibility held by believers that God exists within creation. And the reasoning that underpins what I shall develop next is based on this line of thinking:

- It is presently not possible for humans to prove God's existence

- But God, if so disposed, could prove his existence in an instant

- Yet God has seemingly chosen not to oblige us by doing this in any scientific or quantifiable way

…which of course begs the question: Why?

'Why might God choose to remain obscure when proof of the Divine would enable all people to believe?'

After all, some might argue that the world would be a better place if people had the assurance of a Creator God who they knew was the author of all life. A God who they knew existed and would be the fulfilment of their future destiny. Well possibly but as we shall see, the issue of Divine obscurity is quite complex. Let us continue to consider why it might be that God chooses to hide from us.

For the remainder of this chapter, I will limit my explanation about God's intentional or unintentional withdrawal from us to those aspects that are essentially God-centric. By this I mean the aspects that relate to decisions God makes to maintain a higher ideal. This is not to suggest that the decisions are beyond our human ability to reason, but rather they require us to adopt a different perspective to understand them. So with this in mind, let us consider:

'Why might God be obscured from us?'

In addressing this question, I will be referring to God's absence from us in terms of 'withdrawal' rather than 'hiding'. My reason for making this distinction is that the term 'hiding' is loaded with meaning as our human understanding leads us to associate it with elements of:

- Guilt – someone has done something wrong
- Play – when people tease or toy with another
- Shyness – which affects our ability to socialise

Of course, the explanations for hiding we see here are problematic in that they relate to the experience of humans and not to the remit of the Divine. Indeed, it is questionable whether an all-powerful being would ever need to behave in any of the ways described. After all, it is unlikely that God feels upset or shy or guilty about creating the universe.

Our semantics in place, let us ask the question, why might God choose to be obscured from us? This is an important question because it seems to challenge what believers understand about God's nature as being proactive and involved with creation. It suggests that the Divine is more like the deist 'Watchmaker God' who has wound the universe like a clock and set it in motion, never to interfere with it again. A more contemporary example would be the Divine Being encountered in the film *2001: A Space Odyssey* who inhabits a white room on the edge of the universe waiting for humans to visit. But if God is not hiding in shame, or playing hard to get, or bashful, how is it that the Divine has become unintentionally obscured from our vision? Moreover, what might be God's reason for doing this?

Well, one explanation (and I am going to limit myself to just this one) is to do with the necessity of creation and the way that God brings the physical universe into being. This idea, developed from a branch of kenotic theology, suggests that God creates a space within himself in which things are enabled to occur in ways that are not subject to the will of the Divine. By this I mean an area or space is created by God where humans are free to make their own choices away from the immediate control of God's perfect will and directive. Consider the following example which I hope will illustrate this.

Imagine that God is defined by the dimensions of a living room. Every square inch of this room is enveloped by the presence of God. As a result, there is no part of the room where God's infinity or perfect will is not evident. In fact, in the expanse of this room, nothing is able to reside other than God or those things that are aligned to the Divine purpose. In short, the environment is God.

However, one day God has an idea and decides to introduce a new thing into the room – human beings. These creatures will have freedom to make their own decisions and act independently from God. But immediately there is a problem: the Divine's will is everywhere in the room, which means humans cannot make these self-determined choices. In an instant, an answer is found and God chooses to vacate a small area of the living room to facilitate a space where these finite realities may exist. In terms of our example we might think of it as something like a fish tank in the room. In this area, the universe and humans may be accommodated in a way that is separate from the infinite rule of God.

In this fish tank world, humans are able to interact and make choices for themselves while the fullness and ultimate will of God remain outside it. God creates and sustains a space in which the Divine Presence is withdrawn, so that other forms of life may exist and flourish. Interestingly, this model might also explain the necessity of why God has to become incarnate (in Jesus Christ) because it is only by this means that the

Invisible God

Divine is able to enter into the world without compromising the freedom of humans. It is perhaps also a very good explanation as to why an all-powerful and infinite God might choose to be revealed in less obvious ways. But how does all of this fit with God's unintentional withdrawal from humanity?

Well, as an all-knowing God would be aware of the limitations of the physical universe and how the Divine can never be adequately revealed through it, so we must conclude that 'acts of creation' will only ever serve as pointers to the greater reality of God. But this does not answer the sceptic who asks the question why God doesn't reveal himself to the world in some other way?

Now I am choosing here to avoid the idea of God's revelation as it is understood as happening in the person and work of Jesus Christ. Instead, I will focus on the consequences for humanity if a full revelation of God were to occur. By this I mean the outcome for us if God obliged our request and entered into the space that has been set aside for our temporal universe to exist. In terms of our example, we are asking what would happen if God displaced the water in the fish tank or broke down its sides, and entered into our physical universe as an infinite being?

Although we are only dealing with a hypothetical model here, which is prone to human ideas of what might happen, I think it is fair to reason that if God entered into our universe, revealing the fullness of the

Divine Presence, the result would be catastrophic. Should the kenotic model I have suggested be correct, it is not unreasonable to surmise that such a move would result in the destruction of our environment:

- Finite things would be enveloped by the infinite reality of God

- Temporal (physical) things would be replaced by a spiritual dimension

More than this, humans would no longer be free to choose and decide for themselves because the unlimited presence and power of God would necessitate that this was the only reality that could occur. Basically, for God to enter our world in any way other than a limited (incarnate) form is likely to herald the end of our universe as the space created for humans to live and grow would be enveloped back into the realm and control of God.

Of course, it is quite likely that God understands this outcome and so does not oblige our desire to be fully revealed in the way we seek. It is even possible that human requests are ignored because God understands that at the exact moment that fullness is revealed to us, everything in our world will be inadvertently assimilated back into the Divine realm. With this in mind, consider another fish tank example.

The feeder and the fish tank

Imagine an environment in which tropical fish are kept – the water is oxygenated, treated and heated to a certain temperature. Now imagine that this tank is created by a person who we shall call the 'feeder'. The feeder takes care to protect the fish and makes the tank in a unique way so that it is almost a completely sealed unit – the only access into the tank is via a minuscule opening at the top where food and oxygen can be supplied to sustain life. As the fish move around the tank, some of them wonder about the existence of the feeder. Some fish observe the shadowy image that feeds them which is distorted through the refraction of the glass. Others think nothing of it, though a few fish mistake their own reflections in the glass, thinking it the image of their provider.

But the fish are unhappy and wonder why the feeder does not reveal himself. The feeder senses the fishes' unhappiness and longs that they understand him through the world that is sustained around them. However, the feeder also knows that there is no way that their request can be met, short of breaking into their world, releasing the water and exposing the fish to an alien environment. So the dilemma facing the feeder is that if he obliges them, the fish will have their answer but their world will be irreparably damaged. Conversely, if the feeder refuses their request, their aquatic world is given time to continue for a while with the possibility that the fish might find their answer by some other means.

The God of the Cruel World

From this example, it will hopefully be seen how God's reluctance to be fully revealed in our world may be motivated by a concern that humanity continues and develops unhindered. But this raises the question: why wouldn't God choose to be revealed in some other way in which the fullness of the Divine presence might be displayed in a different form? Of course, believers are quick to remember instances in the Bible where God has been revealed through a burning bush or pillar of fire. However, sceptics are as quick to point out that these episodes have proved to be exceptions to the rule in that they have not been repeated since. This requires us to question why God might not reveal himself in some sort of acceptable lesser measure – a blazing angel or the like.

One possible answer is that even the smallest measure of God's presence in the world might be totally overwhelming for humanity. Consider a different example taken from the television series *'Star Trek'*. In this programme, the ship's crew always take care not to interfere with the delicate balance of life they encounter on other planets. They do this by taking steps to safeguard the environments they visit, keeping inhabitants safe from experiencing and seeing things (particularly technology) that might be in advance of what they can understand and use. The crew's overriding concern is that nothing happens to cause the people harm or damage the progress they might be making.

Now, in applying such thinking to God's revelation to humanity, a similar case might be argued that rather than being passively indifferent to our pleas for proof, the Divine might actually be acting in ways that are for our greater good. God might be taking care not to overexpose humanity to the Divine presence if he knows this would inadvertently cause people to change in the light of this experience. And because the revelation of the Divine reality would be likely to have a consequence, particularly in regard to the issue of freewill, we become aware of how easily our humanity would be compromised by such an event. This revelation of God would affect both individuals and their communities as people would change in the way they think and act.

This brings us to the end of our initial examination of these five questions. Hopefully, you will have gained a better understanding of these issues and objections, though it is just as likely you will have also found that there are no simple answers to these issues – just better questions. Consider next, a few personal thoughts on these issues and the nature of sceptic/believer debate.

Part 3
Thinking Ahead

9 Not a Conclusion
(Just a few thoughts)

This is my second attempt at writing this chapter. My first attempt resulted in the postscript that follows next, which is more of an observation about sceptics and believers than anything else. This means that there is no conclusion to the five tough questions outlined in the previous chapters. Not that this is a problem for me, because I informed you right at the start that I have no wonderful answers to these issues, just different questions and other ways of thinking around the subject.

One of the main difficulties I have with writing any sort of conclusion to this book is that it goes against the whole principle of the Tough Questions Forum, which anticipates that each person will arrive at their own understanding of these issues. I also imagine that any conclusion I might have will be unsatisfactory for a number of people because it is unlikely that everyone will think and reason in exactly the same way I do. Moreover, in a few years when I have had opportunity to consider these issues at greater length, it is quite possible that I might not agree with the conclusions I reach today.

Of course, sometimes the problem is not with the conclusion itself, but with the particulars of each person's experience and how this dictates the way that evidence is considered. I will say more about this in the next chapter. Other times, it could simply be that people are at different places in their understanding of the subject. What one person might hail as an 'absolute masterpiece', is just as likely dismissed by another who considers it amateurish. Not that this is a problem, because we all owe a debt of gratitude to the many theologians and philosophers who have wrestled hard with these issues over the years in order that we might gain a better understanding.

The second difficulty that I have in forwarding a conclusion is that it catapults me into the same position as the 'pluralist narrator' (encountered in chapter 7) whose understanding about God is done in such a way that it is in advance of everyone else in the world – which is certainly not me, nor my intention! If anything, I would hope that my desire to avoid 'glib' answers might qualify me among those who are seeking to discover truth, rather than the few who claim to possess a monopoly of it already and deal in complete (but unsatisfactory) explanations.

Now, in an attempt to appease those who will feel cheated by finding no conclusion at the end of this book, I will make a concession and outline a couple of personal questions and challenges that I have been left with from investigating these issues. I anticipate these will more likely resonate with believers because there are no clear and obvious answers that can be given. Consider then, my understanding as someone who speaks from a faith perspective – in reflective terms, this is my 'thesis' to which you are welcome to bring your own 'antithesis' to bear.

Not a Conclusion

Let me start by saying that I have no issue with the idea of a Creator God who acts in loving ways towards the world. However, I do think that there is scope for considering how this is understood for it seems that our environment is prone to events that we often perceive as cruel or evil. I am referring here to things like natural disasters and illnesses, rather than issues of moral evil where humans might be held culpable for their action or inaction. Given that the world is physically compromised in this way, I am left with two immediate questions:

1. **How did the earth become such a dangerous place to live?**

2. **Was it always God's intention to introduce humans into a potentially hostile world?**

My own understanding of the first question is that there are two strands that need to be considered here. Firstly, the idea of how the world was a safe environment but somehow became compromised so that it was no longer the perfect place that God intended for humanity. Secondly, the notion that we inhabit a world that God has made for us but which seems to be constructed in such a way that conflict occurs within it as part of its design specification – by this I mean a world in which hurricanes, tectonic movement, bacteria, gravity, and such like are all necessary to facilitate human life. The same features which may also threaten human existence. Indeed, as I write this down I am aware of a different question:

119

'Is our world better explained by consideration of both ideas together?'

What I mean by this is that rather than the truth being arrived at through only one of these explanations, maybe there is scope for both ideas to be considered together. In other words, the explanation that God designed the world in such a way that humans might live and develop (while at risk from a range of other things) may be considered alongside ideas about creation being compromised by a spiritual conflict. The two positions are not opposite but rather two explanations of the how and why the world is the way it is in regard to natural and moral evil. Indeed, this line of thinking seems to work for the second question by considering how spiritual rebellion may have occurred at a time after God had introduced life into the world – a conflict which affected life in ways that God may not have anticipated when he first devised 'project earth' and set it into motion. Again, another chapter in a different book!

Obviously, there is lot more that could be said here but I think it is enough to be going on with. Consider next a short postscript about sceptics and believers which has been informed by my observations of people who have taken part in the Tough Questions Forum.

10 Postscript
(Sceptics and believers)

Well, you did it! You reached the end of the book. You have looked at five of the toughest questions and have come out of it with some answers, or at least some different ways of thinking about these issues. Now, let me be the first to congratulate you because I know getting this far is not an easy thing to do. I say this because what most sceptics and believers usually discover when they participate in the Tough Questions Forum is that cherished ideas and thinking can become quite fragile when exposed to stronger explanations and arguments. These new ideas may cause the individual to rethink their previous position in the light of what they now believe and understand about God.

Often, the believer is challenged in ways they did not anticipate at the start. Perhaps they have always held to orthodox explanations but now have to rethink what they believe in the light of more compelling ideas. Other times, it is the sceptic who is challenged. The atheist may now recognise that this term no longer adequately describes what they think and believe and they may see themselves as maybe more of a rationalist.

Whatever place you find yourself in as you reach the end of this initial part of the journey, please be encouraged that you have begun to engage with the real issues about life in this world. You resisted the strong temptation to put down the book at the early stage and instead you have chosen to engage with material and ideas that will have been challenging to you and the position you started from. Having travelled this far, might I encourage you to journey a little further. Keep thinking about these issues by reading and researching around the subjects even more. Don't just read books that support what you currently believe, but read other material that is challenging to what you think so that you can be fully equipped to discuss these topics with those who have questions. At the end of the book (p145) you will see that I have made a few suggestions as to how you might go about this. But before that, I would like to share something I sense might be helpful for both sceptic and believer alike: a postscript from the forum itself.

Over the years, I have led many discussion groups on the Tough Questions Forum and listened to many sceptics and believers explaining their different ideas and positions. However, the most important observation that I have made in all this time is that the sceptic and believer are not different but actually the same.

I first became aware of this one evening when a sceptic in the group challenged a believer and accused them of being irrational. The discussion continued and I wandered off in my thoughts, pondering whether the person was making an irrational claim in the light of the evidence that had been presented. As I thought about the arguments of both people, I suddenly arrived at my 'Eureka!' moment: I began to see that both were being quite rational in their thinking. The only difference was that the believer's rationality was informed by a weightier factor: their previous experience of having met and engaged with God.

As I have thought more about this in recent times, it seems to me that both sceptics and believers exercise rational thinking in their debates. Indeed, both also make excellent arguments to support what they truly believe. The sceptic argues in ways to support the belief that the Divine does not exist, while the believer makes the case that God is real and involved with creation.

Common to both positions is the issue of what the individual has experienced. The sceptic who has not (or at least, not yet) experienced God, reasons out of the experience of not having had an encounter with the Divine, while the believer reasons out of what they hold to be their experience of God. The rational flux that occurs in the middle is not as important as the issue of 'experience' which determines how people approach the evidence in front of them and form their arguments and what positions they adopt. Of course, the thing that actually separates them is the issue of God's 'revelation', which affects the way that each person thinks and acts. People who have encountered God (in whatever way this has occurred) are likely to think and act differently from those who have had no 'revelation'. Indeed, it must be considered that should the sceptic, at a later date, experience some 'revelation' of God, his or her position could change in an instant!

Since beginning to explore these tough questions, my thinking is different today than when I first started. Usually I begin the opening session of each Tough Questions Forum by explaining what I think will happen over the duration of the course, telling the group that they will be sadly disappointed if they have come expecting me to answer all their questions.

Instead, I tell them that although the forum will not do this for them, it is quite likely that they will emerge with a different mindset which will equip them to answer and formulate better questions for themselves. These questions will get to the heart of what many people struggle with in the world today.

Many people genuinely want to believe in a God but cannot stomach the absurdities that are presented to them by believers. Often, these absurdities are advanced by well-meaning followers who quite happily posit that God is capable of both good and evil because it allows them to maintain a model of the Divine as all-seeing, all-knowing and all-powerful in the midst of terrible tragedies around the world. And of course these tragedies include instances where people die in horrific ways or at an early point in life. This can be a hardship made considerably worse when incorrect ideas about the Divine are advanced. Ideas that propose these events can be explained as being part of God's good and perfect will. My own understanding of these events is that they occur outside of God's intention and purpose for the world, because God's overriding desire for people is to experience goodness in this life. Moreover, I believe God grieves with all of us when such tragedies occur.

From what I have just outlined it will be apparent that I believe God is kind and loving. I also recognise that this reality of the Divine is often obscured by the cruelty and hardships of the world in which we live. A problem made even more difficult by unhelpful ideas about God as the arbiter of human pain and suffering – ideas often propagated by people who consider themselves believers.

Hopefully, this book will have helped you to think through these issues from a number of perspectives so that you have arrived at some reasoned answers for yourself. My prayer is that you advance in your understanding so that you may know and experience liberating truth. I also pray that you may be spared glib Christian answers and that your 'Eureka!' moments may be many as you seek answers to the tough questions. May God bless you in your endeavours!

11 Reflection Sheets

Moral Evil (p39-50)
Why doesn't God do something about evil people in the world?

Before you start to read this chapter, record your own understanding of this issue in the space below:

(thesis)

Having read the chapter on 'Moral Evil', what ideas (if any) have challenged your thinking in regard to this subject?

(antithesis)

Natural Evil (p51-69)
Why does God allow natural disasters to occur?

Before you start to read this chapter, record your own understanding of this issue in the space below:

(thesis)

Having read the chapter on 'Natural Evil', what ideas (if any) have challenged your thinking in regard to this subject?

(antithesis)

Death and Illness (p71-84)
Why did my friend have to die?

Before you start to read this chapter, record your own understanding of this issue in the space below:

(thesis)

Having read the chapter on 'Death and Illness', what ideas (if any) have challenged your thinking in regard to this subject?

(antithesis)

World Religions (p85-99)
Do all religions lead to God?

Before you start to read this chapter, record your own understanding of this issue in the space below:

(thesis)

Having read the chapter on 'World Religions', what ideas (if any) have challenged your thinking in regard to this subject?

(antithesis)

Invisible God (p101-113)
Is it possible to prove God's existence?

Before you start to read this chapter, record your own understanding of this issue in the space below:

(thesis)

Having read the chapter on 'Invisible God', what ideas (if any) have challenged your thinking in regard to this subject?

(antithesis)

12 Questions for Group Discussion

Moral Evil (p39-50)

Why doesn't God do something about evil people in the world?

Q1) What are your initial thoughts about this chapter? Does it help in making sense of evil and if so, how?

Q2) Can every occurrence of human evil be traced back to the issue of freewill? How reasonable is it to think that humans have a propensity to do evil from their early years?

Q3) How much to you agree or disagree with the statement (below) made by Eugene Borowitz?

'Any God who could permit the holocaust, who could remain silent during it, who could hide his face whilst it dragged on ... was [and is] not worth believing in.'

Q4) Do you believe that evil is the logical necessity of human freewill? If not, what else might explain it?

Q5) Is it fair to describe evil outcomes as the rejection of good? Why?

Natural Evil (p51-69)
Why does God allow natural disasters to occur?

Q1) How do you understand natural disasters? Do you believe God to be responsible for these events?

Q2) Allowing for the positive and negative aspects of many things in our world (for example, gravity), how feasible is it to think the world was ever perfect in the way that some believe it to have been?

Q3) How helpful or unhelpful is the idea that tectonic movement is a necessary part of development and maintenance of human life on this planet? Do you think this explanation lets God 'off the hook' in regard to natural disasters or are there other things to be considered?

Q4) Might humans be thought of as partly culpable for adding to the outcome of natural disasters by living in areas prone to these events? Is human freewill a factor here?

Q5) What do you think about Gregory Boyd's idea that natural disasters are part of a world compromised by evil through spiritual forces acting against God?

Death and Illness (p71-84)
Why did my friend have to die?

Note to leader and group – sensitivity will be needed in the discussion of these issues as it is possible that one or more members of the group may know someone who is suffering illness, or even be experiencing this for themselves. Similarly, it is very likely that most people will have experienced bereavement at some point in their life and may still be affected by this in ways that make discussion of these issues not such an easy thing to do.

Q1) Is it fair for people to blame God for illness and diseases in the world?

Q2) What is your thinking in regard to the orthodox belief that death and illness are related to human rebellion away from God?

Q3) Can the benefits of bacteria in our bodies be seen as outweighing any negative outcomes that may occur from other types of bacteria?

Q4) Do the issues of human death and illness become redundant with the idea of resurrection and an after-life?

World Religions (p85-99)
Do all religions lead to God?

Q1) What do you think about the pluralist idea that all religions are attempts to understand the same God? How convincing is the argument the pluralist makes?

Q2) Given the variety of religions in the world and the different ways that each worships and understands its own particular revealed truth, how feasible is it that all of them are right in what they believe?

Q3) What are your feelings and thoughts in regard to exclusivist claims that

  a) God chooses only one way to be revealed?

  b) God only accepts one way for people to be restored back into relationship?

Q4) How reasonable or unreasonable is the (Christian) inclusivist idea that all religions are saved though the atoning work of Christ?

Invisible God (p101-113)
Is it possible to prove the existence of God?

Q1) Is it ever possible for humans to prove God in a consistent (rational) way that will convince others of this reality?

Q2) How reasonable is the idea that God chooses to be limited within our world in order that human freewill is not compromised by the absolute certainty of the Divine's existence?

Q3) What do you think about the idea of a space being created within the infinite presence of the Divine so that a human environment might be enabled to exist?

Q4) How helpful is the example of the 'feeder' and the fish tank?
Is this illustration useful in explaining the reasons why God does not oblige our request to be fully revealed within our world?

Q5) Thinking about how God chooses not to be fully revealed within our world, does this explain the necessity for the Divine to become incarnate?

13 Further Reading and Research

So you have reached the end of the book and your interest has been sufficiently piqued to the extent that you would like to read and research these issues further – so what next?

Well, my advice to those who read the book by themselves is to now go and search for people who you can discuss these issues with as I believe this type of activity will be useful in developing a more rounded understanding of how others view these issues – possibly you could use a blog where all else fails?

For those who have discussed the issues with others, my advice is to keep on engaging with these questions by reading around this subject even more. Of course, this will be a trial and error process for most people as there is a plethora of material in bookshops and on the internet. Often, these materials offer simplistic explanations to these questions – the real research skill will be the way you are able to filter through the results of search engines to find sites that are usefully addressing these issues. Although I can think of a number of books that people may find useful, there is not enough space to list them all here. Instead, may I suggest my own Tough Questions website as a starting point (which I will be developing further) where you will find links to some sites I have found useful and a few books I have read or would recommend. All the best.

www.toughquestions.org

References

[1] Variations of Edmund Burke quote in http://tartarus.org/~martin/essays/burkequote.html

[2] E Borowitz *'The Mask that Jews Wear'* (Simons & Schuster, New York 1973) p99

[3] D Hume's treatment of the Epicurean question: http://www.massline.org/PhilosDog/E/Evil.htm

[4] MW Myers *Brahman: 'A Comparative Theology'* (Curzon, 2001) p192

[5] CS Lewis *'The Four Loves'* (Harcourt, 1988)

[6] JP Sartre, *'Being and Nothingness'* (New York: Pocket Books, 1984), p478

[7] NIV Bible Romans 8v22

[8] M Palmer *'The Question of God'* (Routledge, 2002) p119

[9] Extract from FMA Voltaire's poem *'All is Well'* (1755) in http://geophysics.tau.ac.il/personal/shmulik/LisbonEq-letters.htm

[10] A Tennyson quote from *'In Memorium A.H.H'* (1850) in http://www.everything2.com/index.pl?node_id=1751122

[11] GA Boyd *'God at War'* (IVP, 1997) p104
[12] ibid p107

[13] *'Tsunami: Where was God?'* (Faith & Belief, 2005 Ch4)

[14] *'New Dictionary of Theology'* (IVP, 1998) p576
[15] *'New Dictionary of Theology'* (IVP, 1998) p135

Other books by this author..

Plausible Alternatives
Bob Eckhard

Was there a global flood during the time of Noah?
Can grass grow on molten lava as creation accounts seem to suggest?
Did Adam exist and if so, is he missing a rib?

In this book, Bob Eckhard takes a rational look at literalist interpretations of the Bible and considers how reasonable these explanations are in the light of what is understood about the world today. A series of interesting outlines looking at Genesis narrative and some suggestions as to what might really be going on.....

(available Spring 2008)

A short book of **Believer Absurdities**
Bob Eckhard

How feasible is it to suggest the earth is 6,000 years old? Are fossils really the work of the devil as some would have us believe?

Is God actually answering believers' prayers when they find an empty space at the busy supermarket car park?

Continuing the quest for better explanations, Bob Eckhard casts a sceptical eye over some of the more questionable ideas that believers have about the way that God and spiritual forces are at work in the world today. Despite its controversial title, the book is an attempt to challenge believers to rationally reflect on ideas and practices that people outside of the church consider absurd – an opportunity to identify the ways in which God is active in the world, yet separate from events that are better explained as happenchance, coincidence or accident….

(available Summer 2008)

www.ingramcontent.com/pod-product-compliance
Ingram Content Group UK Ltd.
Pitfield, Milton Keynes, MK11 3LW, UK
UKHW041436180426
11947UKWH00007B/482